# REASONS FOR QUILTS

*An Inspiring Treasury of Quilts and Their Stories*

By Edyta Sitar

With Judith Stern Friedman

Laundry Basket Quilts

1

# Acknowledgements

*I am so grateful for everyone who has joined me on this bookmaking journey:*

*To my quilting friends, buddies, and groupies:* My stash is full because of you. Like a human quilt, you have blanketed me with support, encouragement, and feedback.

*To my family:* You have shared my innermost hopes and dreams and have rallied me to rise to my best. Without hesitation, you have accompanied me in all my adventures and showered me with love and continuous praise.

*To my dear Michael:* Since the day we dreamed of this book, you have been my most avid fan and supporter. With your steady hand and focus on making every detail right, you have showcased my quilts in such beautiful light. I am so thankful and blessed to have you by my side in business and in life.

*To Judy:* In words, you have captured my stories and my feelings and have done the impossible, like catching butterflies in an open field. I truly am thankful and believe in some way, that the reason for making my quilts was to meet you.

*To Kayleen:* Your hard work, graphic talent, and patience show in these meticulously layered pages. In assembling words, quilts, and graphics so seamlessly, you have created a beautifully wrapped gift for quilters and quilt lovers.

*To Moda and United Notions staff:* In your endless endorsement of my work, and in manufacturing the fabrics that bring my quilts alive, you have allowed me to live my dream of designing.

*To Grandma Anna, My Mother-In-Law, and My Mother:* You have been my role models as wives, mothers, quilters, and women—and have given me the gift of your caring and nurturing, wisdom, and strength to take on the world with open eyes and mind.

This book was designed, produced, and published by Sitar Family Traditions LLC, DBA:
Laundry Basket Quilts, 16860 L Drive North, Marshall, MI 49068
www.laundrybasketquilts.com

**Publisher:** Sitar Family Traditions LLC, Laundry Basket Quilts
**Quilt Design:** Edyta Sitar and Quilts from Sitar Family Collection
**Author:** Edyta Sitar, Laundry Basket Quilts
**Contributing Author:** Judith Stern Friedman
**Art Director:** Kayleen Hardy, Hardy Design Studio
**Photography:** Michael Sitar, Laundry Basket Quilts

Library of Congress Control Number: 2011910322
ISBN 13: 978-0-9836688-0-0

This book is printed on acid-free paper.
Printed in China.
10 9 8 7 6 5 4 3 2 1

# Opening the Trunk...
## Table of Contents

# REASONS FOR QUILTS

W a t c h i n g ,
*wondering,*
p o n d e r i n g ,
*playing.*
I am the little girl who never grew up.
*My thread* like a kitten's ball of string,
*My thimble*, a dolly's drinking cup.

Like a box of crayons,
*my fabric* a treasure,
*My needle*, a brush to paint my way.
Through growing,
*loving, marrying and mothering,*
I document *every celebrated day.*

Life gives us *reasons for making quilts,*
By way of *being, bonding, and sharing,*
Not product, but process is *the inspiration*
For making these *timeless icons* of caring.

—Written for *Reason for Quilts*
by Edyta Sitar and Judith Stern Friedman

# Life Beneath the Threads

Every quilt is a piece of art—but the true art lies among its layers.
Deep beneath the colors and patterns are meanings that embrace the fabric of our lives.
Through cutting, assembling, and painstaking stitching, we dream of our quilts in their finished form. Yet the true beauty lies in the making of quilts. In the hundreds of pieces that teach us patience; in mistakes that make us a bit more humble; and through setbacks that spur even greater resolve, quilting both reflects and shapes our being.

## For every quilt, there is a reason:

### TO VALIDATE OURSELVES

We create souvenirs of our existence, expressing our spirit through our
fabric choices, colors, patterns, threads, and stitches.

### TO HONOR MILESTONES

and even to mourn them, we create quilts to capture our joys and ease our pains.

### TO HONOR FRIENDSHIPS AND CLOSE COMMUNITY

We look for ways to make our own fun, find connection, and revel in shared experience.

### TO RECOGNIZE THE HUMAN CONDITION

As tributes to our nation's momentous events, valued leadership,
and prized personal freedoms, we make quilts to honor our place in the world.

### TO CREATE A MEANS FOR GIVING BACK

We use quilts to help relieve people's suffering, to raise funds for important social causes,
and ultimately, to foster a warmer society.

### TO MARK IMPORTANT SPIRITUAL OCCASIONS

We make quilts in reverence to our faith and the sacred holiday rituals that surround it.

### TO ACKNOWLEDGE THE AWE IN EVERY DAY

We translate our experiences with nature and the seasons to capture their precious fleeting moments.

### TO CONTINUE A RICH AMERICAN TRADITION

Folding them gracefully on the couch, spreading them across a bed, or hanging them proudly on the wall,
we make utilitarian quilts for decorating our homes and warming our hearts.

All these reasons for making quilts are my inspiration for writing this book.
How can a tiny needle and thread hold such power to express how we feel and what we do?
*How can a simple piece of fabric change lives—and become a canvas for life itself?*

As you join me on this journey through *Reasons for Quilts,* consider not only the stories quilts tell,
but also the countless people they touch. In joy, sadness, abandon, acceptance, pain, suffering, worship and wonder—
quilts capture human emotion and experience. And so people will always have reason to make quilts,
and we will always have reason to treasure them.

Carol Sitar

Edyta Sitar with
her mother, Kristina

Grandpa John and Grandma Anna Sitar

*This book is dedicated to Grandma Anna—*
*and all the grandmothers of the world—for their unconditional open arms, giving hearts,*
*and immeasurable sacrifice—and for teaching us lessons that endure through generations.*

# A Patchwork of Memories

*On a memorable day when I was four years old, my relationship with textiles began—*
*although it just as easily could have ended…*

There I stood at our living room window, watching my mother finesse the folds as she hung her
just-finished homespun drapes. In my eyes, these larger-than-life window dresses were as thrilling as any fashion show.
Framing nature outside while creating a stunning altar inside, dramatic flowers on a textured weave beckoned
me almost magnetically. I watched as my mother gently patted the pleats, smoothed the ruffles,
and set them just so, and I yearned to feel what she was feeling.

At an opportune moment when she stepped away, I stepped up to take my cut, snipping a
piece of this woven wonder. I believed I could make something just as beautiful.

But the fantasy stopped as quickly as it started when my mother returned to see what I had done…

She could have scolded me for cutting her designer drapes; but instead, she replaced the
fabric in my hand with a more acceptable stack of scraps.

Quietly, she repaired the severed curtain panel, and I went off to fashion my stash into a blankie for my doll.
My mother's handmade curtains, complete with lasting "scar," hung in our house for almost 40 years.

Today, when my mother points to the curtains, I know she has the upper hand. But truly, I open my hands to her for
recognizing my love of fabric even then. I grew up expressing myself with thread and needle, sewing skirts,
purses, pillowcases, curtains and later, even elaborate wedding gowns.

## Rocking the Needle

All these projects prepared me well for my later entrée into quilting, just after I married my husband, Michael.
As young, innocent newlyweds in the early 1990s, we knocked at the door of Michael's grandmother Anna, who agreed
to let us stay in her home while we arranged our lives. I remember entering her intimate kitchen, nose-to-nose
with freshly baked bread and then getting to taste it on her blue willow dishes.

But Grandma Anna had bigger plans beyond this warming welcome: "If you're going to live here,
you're going to quilt here," she warned. I had grown up in a modest home in Poland and had never seen a quilt before,
nor had I ever known anyone who quilted. As I turned to avoid her penetrating gaze, color in the living room drew my
eye to a blanket spread between two chairs. "Isn't Grandma a little too old to be making a tent?"
I thought, thinking this woman must still have some child in her.

I soon learned, however, that the tent was a quilt and that quilting was Anna's personal pride. She often churned out
a coverlet a week to raise money for her church. That very tent was the top on which I learned to quilt—before
Anna even taught me to piece together my first quilt top. We stitched. We talked. We shared our daily trials.
As Anna encouraged me as a young new wife, she also taught me confidence in newfound skills.
We became companion quilters, but more importantly, we bonded as friends.

As I sat directly across from Anna, she taught me how to rock a needle—and not to rock the family boat.
We expressed our closeness through the quilts we made, admiring each finished heirloom on a clothesline in
Anna's backyard. And then we folded them into a laundry basket, until the next delivery to the church.

Soon, I found myself expecting a child, glowing with reason to make a quilt of my own. Now I could funnel what
Anna had taught me into a top that marked my motherhood. Yet the child in me was still very much alive.
Fueled by the flutter of movement inside, I filtered my excitement into each piece of fabric. Bright,
colorful prints and happy patterns foretold the little life that would soon change mine.

Folklore suggests that
society expected young, unmarried
pioneer women to make quilts.
But for wedded wives, the standard
eased to smaller, baby quilts.
Occupied with labor-intensive household
chores, women could not spare the time
to make big quilts; so they adapted the
larger patterns they knew to model less
demanding versions of the same.

# HUSH, LITTLE BABY

*We make quilts for tiny miracles—fragile, innocent,*
*still yet to understand—to wrap, protect, and warm through and through.*

# 1. DOUBLE BROKEN STAR LOG CABIN
(Small: 39"x39"; Large: 87"x87")

One of my personal favorite patterns is the timeless Log Cabin, with its classic red center square symbolizing hearth and home. Assembling the pieces is like building a cabin, piecing dark and light strips as if layering the walls.

Both constructions here consist of 64 total blocks, including 32 squares of half-light and half-dark logs; 16 squares of all light logs; and 16 squares of all dark logs. While the layout of the colors is the same in both quilts—using men's and women's shirtings for the lighter fabrics, and brown and cocoa tones for the darker fabrics—the large logs are twice as wide as the baby logs, yielding 9-inch and 4-1/2-inch blocks, respectively.

## 2. BUBBLE GUM, BUBBLE GUM (45"x45")

As America's pioneers viewed children as small adults, they designed their coverlets accordingly, typically based on 6-inch blocks. A mother could have fashioned this traditional Turkey Tracks pattern from her leftover brown dresses and clothing scraps. Set in alternating blocks of bubble-gum pink, the mesmerizing colors caress babies to sleep.

# 3. DAYBREAK (40"x40")

As young girls grew older, child quilts were the means for showcasing their sewing skills. This quilt offers the opportunity to "stitch and shine." Bursts of double eight-pointed stars frame a pot of primitive flowers, blooming in shades of royal blue (for protection), red (for passion), and green (for abundance)—reminiscent of traditional Pennsylvania Dutch colors. Reverse prairie points take exquisite detail up to the quilt's finished edges.

## 4. TIC-TAC-TOE (41"x41")

Oh, to be a kid again! Lost in endless childhood games, we changed the rules, jumped the lines, drew with chalk, and grabbed for jacks. In the end, who won or lost didn't matter, as long as we were playing together. My favorite game was Tic-Tac-Toe, the simple game of X's and O's, which is my reason for this quilt. Half- and quarter-square triangles and squares meet in a face-off of scrappy browns, beiges, rusts, and reds. As every block is a winning combination, let's call this one "cat's game."

## 5. LOLLIPOP (40"x40")

Like a child in a candy store, my eyes light up when swatches of new fabric land on my doorstep. My Dreaming in Color collection of soft batiks is still among my favorite fabrics and the inspiration for this petite Dresden Plate variation. Popular in the 1920s and 1930s, and honoring the valued German porcelain, Dresden Plate reflects women's love of embellishment in home décor. Here, the traditional pattern turns modern in brightly colored wheels, finished with yellow appliquéd center circles. The result: a wall-size spread of "candy" one can almost taste.

# 6. MY FAVORITE THINGS
(47"x52")

Sometimes my children ask for proof that I was once a child. This signature quilt speaks of the things I loved as a little girl. From family and prayers to cookies and kittens, hand-written words on center squares call attention to what makes me smile. I've even left some empty spaces to remind us that deep down,

*we're still growing up.*

# 7. LITTLE BASKET (42"x55")

New friendship is like a baby: You care for it, cradle it, and put pieces of yourself into nurturing it. When I met my friend, Dominick, we were both finding our way—navigating a new community—and now, together, we found connection through quilting.

We each made 92 three-inch blocks: little baskets that would capture our joys, trials, successes, and the secrets we shared. Giving half to the other and keeping the other half for ourselves, we each made a baby quilt to honor our friendship. I set my baskets in a zigzag pattern of poison green and bubble gum pink to show how seamlessly we fit together. Now, every time I see my quilt, I know exactly which baskets Dominick pieced. I'm reminded of the friendship we've woven so tightly—and the baskets we still have yet to fill.

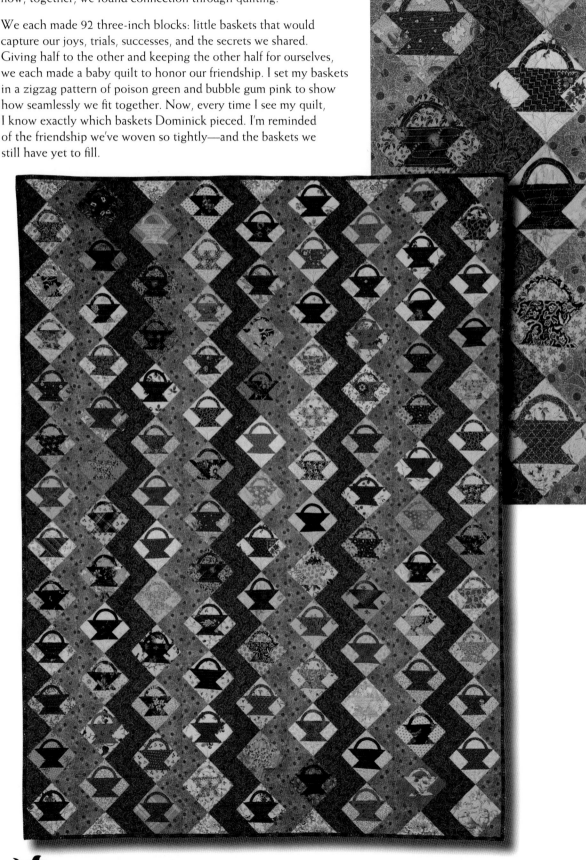

# 8. CROSSROADS (54"x54")

Representing the transitional time in my life from childbearing to child rearing, this quilt departs from the Log Cabin pattern. Starting with an oversized center "hearth," I layered logs of sectioned browns and pinks—and when I was done, the pieces revealed a secondary pattern: modeled brown stars on a field of pink. The design lent itself to sashing and cornerstones, which break away from traditional Log Cabins.

The story behind this quilt begins with my mother-in-law, Carol, who came to visit for afternoon tea. As we casually sat at the kitchen table, she gently pushed a package my way. I untied the ribbon and uncovered the box to reveal a quilt—a baby quilt!

But I was not expecting, nor was I planning, as Michael and I had completed our family. Two girls and a boy were enough for us to handle. But my mother-in-law had other intentions: She wanted to even the boy-girl score by giving me a blue and yellow quilt that somehow would fulfill her wish for another grandson.

The lesson: Delivering a baby requires much more than simply receiving a quilt. For those who hope for a new generation, perhaps wrapped up in the giving of quilts is the unspoken blessing of fertility.

*P.S. Coincidentally, Carol's prophecy did come true: Another grandson was born to Michael's sister several years later.*

When children show an interest in holding a
needle and thread, what an opportune time to
teach them how to quilt. Without worry that the
lines will not be straight, that the fabrics don't
match, or the top won't lie flat, children will
stitch with complete abandon. Innocent of the
pressures to piece a perfect quilt, they'll glow in
the chance to be making it with you. They'll quiet
in the calming feel of the fibers, wiggle in wonder
of the brilliant colors, and beam when you
snip the final dangling threads.

# PLAYING WITH DOLLS

*We make quilts to capture our lives in miniature worlds.*
*As our dolls experience the same pleasures and pains, quilts give us reason to practice*
*compassion. We use quilts to comfort our dolls when they are sick, warm them when*
*they're cold, and secure them when tucking them into bed at night.*

*But the true reward of making doll quilts is in passing on the pleasures of sewing with a child.*

BOISTEROUS BEAR

# 9. PRETTY IN PINK (17"x17")

In making a quilt with any child, choosing the fabric is particularly thrilling, as eyes light up at the myriad of choices. In the end, the child chooses colors and patterns that reflect the essence of his or her character. As in the past, strips and logs are the easiest beginnings, as they allow straight sewing with no curves or added stitching. Starting in the center with a basic star block, strips upon strips come together seamlessly. It doesn't matter how straight the lines, as long as the pieces meet at the edges.

My daughter, Delfina, is a fan of pink—a reflection of her feminine, delicate spirit—which drives the look of this simple stripped quilt. She stitched it when she was just eight years old.

# 10. ANNA'S BANANA QUILT (19"x19")

The child's age, dexterity, and maturity gauge the need for adult involvement. While Delfina sewed independently on the machine, I helped four-year-old Anna make her quilt. Grounded in fun and quirky banana yellows, this version reflects Anna's animated spirit. It follows the same stripping method as Delfina's, but the fabric completely changes the look.

Doll quilts finish with a smaller, delicate binding to reflect their miniature scale. In some cases, even a single quilt block, originally designed for a full-size quilt, is enough to make a cozy doll quilt. Often, quilters work up single-block samplers to see how fabrics and colors work together. Instead of designating these squares as stash, they're easily framed and bound into doll quilts.

# 11. MONKEY WRENCH (26"x26")

As Delfina and Anna both enjoyed their custom quilts, my third child, Michael, had to be in the picture. Quietly interested in my skill, watching from afar—and then closer up—he wanted to see this magical machine that was capable of creating such beautiful blankets.

Boys are equally inspired by textiles, and are just as interested in the sewing tools. And so we worked on a quilt just for Michael. In hopes of creating an appropriate pattern, I explored what I knew about this inquisitive little boy: gentle, curious, and always questioning, trying to understand the way things work. From using his tools to take the knobs off my doors to driving trucks—and driving me crazy—Michael had a yen for building things and promptly taking them apart.

The monkey wrench pattern is the perfect expression of Michael's mechanical mind. Also popular in the past for masculine interests, this nine-block construction engages busy minds. Set in light blue and beige tones, the colors reflect traditional boy preferences.

## 12. FOREVER BLISS
(9"x6")

As dolls fulfill our romantic dreams, a quilt must be at the ready for the wedding. Just as pioneers brought their dowries to the altar, so must we offer up heirlooms of value. Dressing our doll bride in the fanciest clothes—often settling for a sparkly evening gown— we fashioned her veil from a length of lace and dreamed of the consummate kiss on "the day." Then, as part of the honeymoon escape, a quilt would bind the new couple physically together.

This traditional 1930s Double Wedding Ring pattern comes to life in miniature form, as it celebrates the union of husband and wife. It also employs a handy quilter's trick: using convenience panels—or preprinted blocks—to eliminate the chore of tiny piecing.

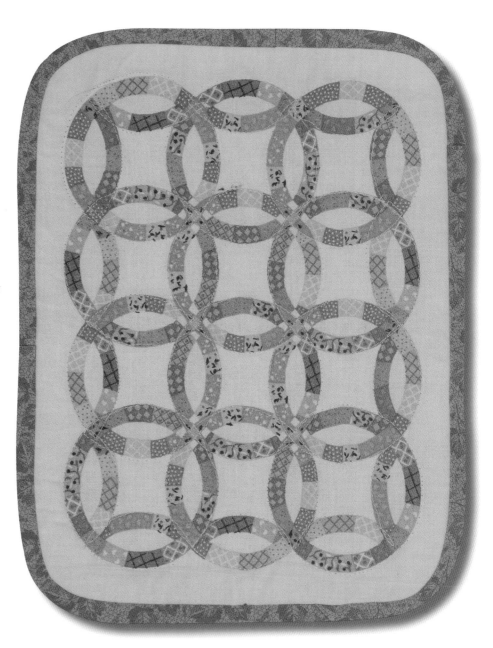

*As children grow up* and live their own fantasy lives, the dolls that entertained them often fade into childhood. Books and other teenage trinkets come to replace their Barbies and Kens. But the quilts they made endure the transition, now assuming new roles as home décor. Perhaps a quilt becomes a dresser scarf, padding the surface under perfume and powder, or grounding a vase and a bunch of fresh-picked flowers. Whether finding new life as a place mat, wall hanging, or a side-table topper, miniature quilts capture innocent memories, and then they move on to tell new stories.

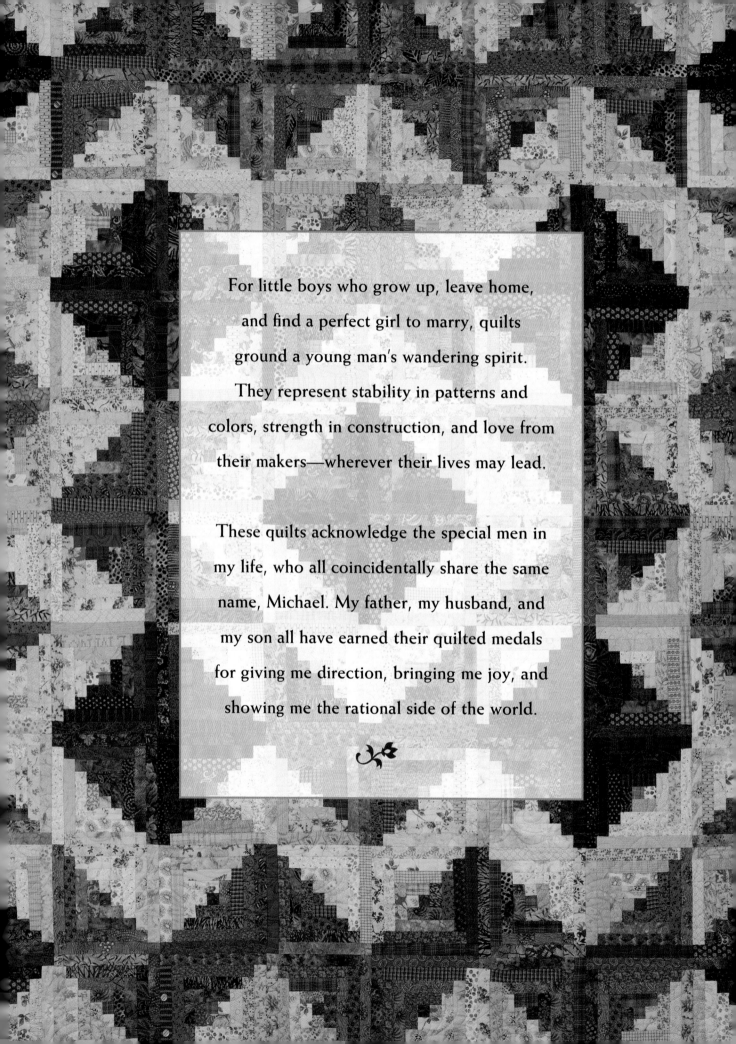

For little boys who grow up, leave home,
and find a perfect girl to marry, quilts
ground a young man's wandering spirit.
They represent stability in patterns and
colors, strength in construction, and love from
their makers—wherever their lives may lead.

These quilts acknowledge the special men in
my life, who all coincidentally share the same
name, Michael. My father, my husband, and
my son all have earned their quilted medals
for giving me direction, bringing me joy, and
showing me the rational side of the world.

# MEMORIES WITH MUSCLE

*We make quilts for the well-meaning men in our lives:*
*For fathers who open our eyes to the world;*
*For husbands who stand by us through life's journey; and*
*For sons who look up to us and learn—and accept us unconditionally.*

*Quilts honor the men who are our protectors, planners, lovers,*
*listeners, breadwinners, bankers, fixers, and friends.*

## 13. COMPASS QUILT (63"x63")

As the middle daughter between two sons, I was always Daddy's little girl, and I knew it for the way he treated me so tenderly. Whether leading us on winding nature walks, making multiple jumps in checkers, or playing the winning card in rummy, Daddy could always find his way out—and he guided me just as wisely and methodically. To this day, I appreciate my father's even temper, honesty, fairness, and pointed ways, which logically play into this compass design.

Nine large compass blocks in bold reds and navy blues come together from Civil War fabrics, set into light reproduction men's shirtings. Using the leftover fabric from the blocks, the zigzag borders reflect my father's energy. The blocks are set into an olive green background, and then finished with binding and hand quilting.

# 14. ROAD BACK HOME (71"x71")

No matter how old we grow, or how distant from our parents, we're always children in their eyes. I designed this quilt for my father's 84th birthday to honor our journey through life together. He watched me grow—stumble, stand, and stumble again—and every time, he was there to pick me up. I knew that wherever in the world I went, I could always come home. As I grew from toddler to teen, wife to mother, and now accomplished quilter, my father has helped me navigate all roads, which were the inspiration for this scrappy quilt.

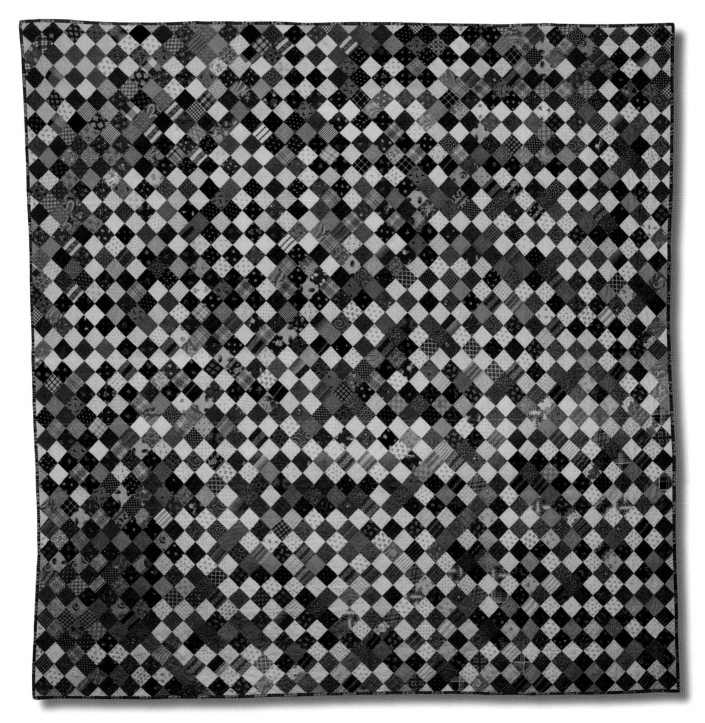

## 15. TREE FARM (55"x72")

For years, Michael's mother comforted him with quilts. His Grandma Anna spoiled him with more quilts. And now it was my turn to assume the role. This quilt embodies my love for Michael and my deepest thanks for his loyalty as a husband, devotion as a father, and boundless compassion as a friend.

This tree of life pattern reflects Michael's fiber as our mighty oak tree. A palette of brilliant autumn colors attracts the eye to fiery reds, translucent yellows, and vivid greens, rooted in dark brown trunks made from paisleys, batiks, and other subtle patterns. Half-square triangles make 18 total blocks, set in a hypnotizing tree farm pattern on a light beige background.

# 16. MAN OF THE HOUSE (75"x75")

Like most men, Michael is our go-to repairman, builder, and toolman extraordinaire—and he does it all without asking for help. If it's broken, he'll fix it; if we need it, he'll build it.  To christen the completion of my quilting studio and barn—which Michael constructed so skillfully by hand—I "built" him this traditional log cabin quilt. The sage blues and browns reflect his masculinity, while touches of pink suggest his softer side.

# 17. THE COUCH QUILT (Hawaiian Delight) (58"x58")

While men typically do not quilt, most appreciate a quilt made for them, out of love and admiration. This quilt, however, was made from frustration, following an instance when Michael did not "behave." Admittedly, every marriage has its insignificant conflicts, but in this case, I was running out of patience. Rather than wasting my breath, I headed out to indulge myself in fabric. Of course, I felt entitled to splurge, to appease my emotions and unruffle my feathers.

Planning and piecing gave me time to practice my patience. The result of my "sessions" was this Hawaiian delight, a pineapple pattern that allowed me to vent and work through my feelings. The "steamy" red center reflects my passion, which gradually turns to happy, cheddar yellow. Combinations of light and dark scraps create a secondary design of floating circles and juicy pineapples. Hand quilting the layers allowed even more time to thoroughly think through my own fault in our tiff. Now we refer to this quilt as "The Couch Quilt," allowing Michael to stay warm, even when (figuratively) relegated to the couch—and now, more often, it comforts him while watching television. Despite his behavior, he always knows I love him and that our differences can yield sweet rewards.

# 18. EVERLASTING WREATH (61"x63")

*Like father, like son* is the story behind this quilt: When our little Michael saw my husband wrapped up in the Couch Quilt, of course, he decided he wanted one, too—despite his ignorance of the story behind it.

I contrived this pineapple variation with a hexagon block and black center triangle. Braided light and dark combinations of strips result in a secondary pattern of big circles resembling everlasting wreaths.

As undoubtedly we all have our moments "on the couch," this quilt inspired me to share my pattern with others. Many quilters have stitched up their own Couch Quilts, which live on armrests in family rooms all over. Deservedly, for the quilting skill involved and the peaceable outcomes they provide, many of these quilts have earned ribbons.

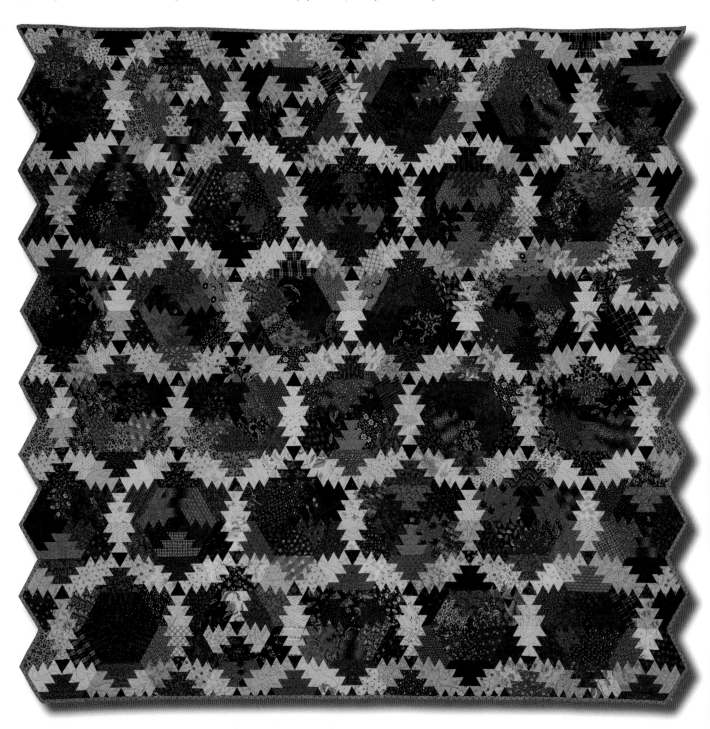

# 19. WESTERN STAR (60"x83")

As our children grew, I continued to make quilts that shadowed their development. The transition from preschool to kindergarten was especially poignant for my youngest Michael and me. As with most children this age, change brews feelings of anxiety and trepidation—shared by both the parents and child. These feelings often express themselves through unplanned, out-of-character behaviors, which was the case when Michael started school.

Though strong in personality like his father, Michael was at first a little lamb, meek and unsure of the pastures ahead. Soon, however, he slid into routine—but perhaps he wasn't quite yet settled.

Shortly after the start of one school day, I answered a phone call from Michael's teacher. She explained that Michael is just like a little sheriff who knows all the rules, but doesn't always follow them. As I listened on the other end of the line, I shrank to hear what she was telling me and didn't want to admit that my son was less than perfect—nor was I willing to discuss it with her.

Rather than face this humbling situation, I told the teacher I didn't understand. I used my language barrier as an excuse and asked her to call Michael's father instead. I had dealt with our two girls prior, and now, I figured, Michael would relate more closely with our son.

What better reason for a quilt than to help the maker resolve her conflict? I designed this Western Star quilt as a tribute to my little sheriff, who has since learned the rules for getting along. The quilt was my strength and personal coach for helping me understand my child. It taught me the patience to see through his behavior, understand his motivations, and help him overcome obstacles. To this day—and despite his rare "outlaw" streaks—Michael represents all that is good.

This traditional six-point star design has remained a favorite since pioneer days. Blues, reds, and browns create waves of color, reminiscent of a child's rolling development. Although each block begins with the same design, changing the colors adds visual impact.

I finished this quilt using milk-white shirting that adds an extra element of detail: Look closely to see small birds in the fabric flying, pecking, and searching for seeds.

Mothers share private moments with daughters,
sisters share secrets, and friends share dreams.
They rely on each other; laugh with each other;
and bask in moments over tea with each other.
They explore, accept, tolerate, and trust to
create unthinkably powerful relationships.

Women are each other's dearest soul mates—
and quilts represent their deepest connections.
When you make a quilt for a friend, you know
she'll value its wisdom and workmanship...
almost as much as she values your company.

# GIRLFRIENDS FOREVER

*Quilts seal the bond between mothers and daughters,*
*sisters, friends, and kindred spirits.*

## 20. ANNA'S QUILT (65"x80")

As the middle daughter between two sons, I was always Daddy's little girl. When we heard the news that I was expecting our second child—and that the baby would be another girl—I rushed to Grandma Anna's house to tell. Grandma was elated that another child would grace our family—and even more joyful that we would name the baby Anna after her.

Up until now, Grandma had rarely made a quilt for anyone, religiously donating her work to the church. Even for relatives who requested a quilt, Grandma would send them off to play Bingo to earn the chance at owning one of her heirlooms. (Yes, Michael played to win our wedding quilt.)

But for baby Anna, the cutting tables turned. Now Grandma offered to make her a special quilt—no Bingo required.

She sent me to the store for fabric, knowing I preferred coordinating colors, as opposed to her signature scrappy style. Grandma got to work with her scissors and template (she never used a rotary cutter or a mat). She sat in her special chair and cut and pieced away, as she listened to the stories on *Days of Our Lives.*

Finally, when she finished, she called me to come over and pick up the precious souvenir: a grandmother's fan pattern arranged in a love circle, with the shapes of lucky four-leaf clovers hand-quilted on each block. In greens, pinks, purples, and lavenders, the pattern predicts the coming of our cutie—with her namesake embroidered for posterity on the back: Great Grandma A. Sitar, September 1997.

# 21. DELFINA'S QUILT (78"x94")

Where siblings all learn the meaning of hand-me-downs, this story considers hand-me-ups.

When Grandma Anna gave me baby Anna's finished quilt, she handed me another tightly wrapped bundle: a generous stack of "leftover" cut shapes that numbered far beyond the pieces she needed. She must have gotten lost in TV and lost count of how much fabric she was cutting.

As I drove home, I understood Grandma's intent. I couldn't give a quilt to Anna without giving the same to her big sister, Delfina. As I held those precut pieces in my hand, I realized my work had been cut out for me.

The artist in me welcomed the challenge of taking the pieces intended for one design and transforming them into another.

Using the pre-cut fabric from Anna's quilt, I folded the tips, and sewed the points together to make Dresden Plates. I appliquéd them to muslin, defined them with dogwood flowers and branches, and then finished with a purple and multi-colored zigzag border.

As soon as I finished the top, I hurried to Grandma Anna's, anxious to show my work to her and my mother-in-law, Carol. We carefully stretched the quilt over the frame and quilted it for Delfina, all three of us together. Now we could deliver two quilts for two sisters—with stitching from the hands of three generations.

## 22. MEDALLION (64"x 74")

My first child, my dear one, my daughter, Delfina, has brought so much joy to my life. Being a parent is often challenging, but the outcomes are so rewarding. As my daughter grows into a young woman, many times, I look up to her and learn from her. The appliquéd basket with flowers at the center symbolizes my daughter's blossoming spirit. Trip around the world frames the center block to show Delfina's desire to travel. Wherever the journey takes her, the quilt will remind her she can always come home.

# 23. MOTHER'S QUILT (69"x63")

After growing up and moving out, I had come a long way since cutting my mother's curtains. With my dad's visit to my house, I wanted to send a handmade gift back with him to my mom. I set to work on a trophy quilt for her, cutting, piecing, and cutting again to impress her with my stitching genius. The more pieces I cut, the more striking the pattern, as I carefully assembled this exquisite top. At last, I wrapped the handmade treasure and sent it, awaiting her reaction.

When my mother opened my gift, she stood looking down with open arms. As a tear slowly dripped down the round of her cheek, she told my dad, "Edyta must be poor! She sewed so many little pieces together." This was the first quilt she had ever seen. In her eyes, a blanket was one piece of fabric, and she thought I couldn't afford the supplies. My mother didn't understand quilting.

Just as I have come a long way, so has society's view of quilting. Pioneer women pieced what fabric they could find—and quilting with scraps was a necessity, not a nicety. But now the fabric industry has evolved in delivering a myriad of colors and textures begging fabric experimentation. With all the possible combinations, today we find pleasure—and even value—in quilting with all sorts of scraps.

# 24. SPECIAL GUEST (68"x55")

When my mother came to visit me for the first time, I tried to make her feel at home: A vase of fresh-picked flowers, clean bathroom towels, and crisp, plumped pillows added to my ritual of tidying the house—and now, a quilt would seal her welcome.

Double eight-point stars set into medallions create this cover in warm reds with brown sashings and touches of delicate pink flowers. The quilt also curiously doubles as a couch quilt, so if my mother does not "behave," she can share a seat with Michael. (See 17. The Couch Quilt, pages 30-31.)

# 25. PINK LEMONADE (60"x80")

Michael especially loved my mother's first visit because she spoiled him with attention. Cooking him meals, serving him snacks, and even folding the napkin on his lap, my mother pulled her son-in-law's strings.

Following three or four days of serving him, she decided now she would serve herself. Mama sauntered into my sewing room, clearly intent on learning to quilt. Though she had taught me to sew years before, now I was the one to show her how. We shopped for fabric, cut pieces, stitched seams, and rocked needles. We didn't discuss our mistakes or regrets. We didn't reveal our disappointments. Instead, we basked in each other's company, simply focused on this fabric art.

"What did you do now?" Michael asked me, sorry he had lost his personal attendant. But I had gained renewed connection with my mom, as we churned out blocks like there was no tomorrow. In quilting, we had lost all track of time and soon, my mom had to return back home. All she left was a stack of blocks and an empty feeling of separation. Quickly I sat down to assemble the blocks, replaying the precious time we spent. In some small way, as if I was a child, I believed the sooner I finished the quilt, the sooner my mother would return to see it and she would be with me again.

## 26. IN FULL BLOOM (72"x63")

Quilts are quite possibly the best way to validate women's close connections. We are like plants in a friendship garden. Lily baskets are the inspiration for this block exchange, where everyone contributes a block to make a quilt, usually in honor of a mutual friend. Reds and light shirtings bloom in flower arrangements, set on point and bordered by fields of blues and yellows.

## 27. BON VOYAGE (86"x86")

*Like friendships that grow* fertile from seed, round robin quilts build layers of pattern, encircling the center. This medallion quilt begins with an appliquéd bird on a blossoming branch, set into a star, and then framed in consecutive tiers. Every quilter adds another border to show her depth of admiration.

# 28. SWAPPING SECRETS (54"x54")

In a fabric exchange, two (or more) friends share the same fabric, but make their own quilts—reinforcing their likenesses, yet revealing their differences. In the end, the quilts become special souvenirs of a point in time when two paths cross. In this case, I arranged my grouping of light and dark fabrics, with triangles on each corner. Just like the paths we share between our yards, the pieces come together in lifelong friendships, destined to live next to each other.

This quilt honors the friendships that happen not necessarily because we choose, but because we connect through our proximity. In the same way that neighbors become close friends, swapping recipes and borrowing sugar, a fabric exchange strengthens ties between quilters.

## 29. GEORGENE (85"x85")

*Friends teach lessons* when we least expect them. A fabric exchange gave me fabric for this quilt—but more importantly, a student gave me inspiration to quilt it.

From the minute Georgene rolled into my classroom, I learned to see quilting from new perspectives. Despite her confinement to a wheelchair, Georgene taught me lessons in self-acceptance, courtesy, confidence, and resilience. Past my reservations about teaching her, Georgene became one of my most outstanding quilting students, always good-natured, patient, and persistent, and truly embracing her happy moments.

For this quilt, we exchanged bundles of 1.5-inch light and dark strips, which when stitched together, became one-inch blocks. The resulting pattern was an Irish chain. In Georgene's spirit, the vintage yellow background fabric cheers up the other colors in this quilt.

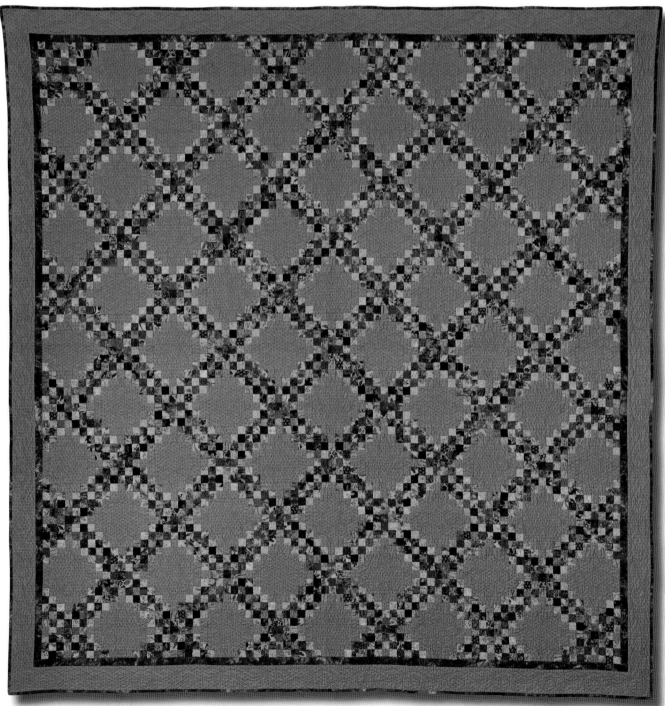

# 30. THE HAND-OFF (72"x72")

Like handing off the baton in a relay race, family members often hand off quilt remnants. Scraps from dresses, pieces from pajamas, grandma's gown, or Uncle Willie's shirts all end up in a patchwork menagerie that somehow never realize completion. These "orphaned" tops are actually quite common, like the one shown here from a woman I once met. "Can you help me finish my mother's quilt?" she asked. Though her hair was silver and her lips were wrinkled, her eyes were those of an innocent child, who simply wanted to preserve her past.

I took the quilt and gave it life, but who's to say whose bed will wear it next? I carried the baton through one leg of this quilt's journey—and passed it on for the next "quilt runner." With luck, it will withstand a long-distance race.

Foretelling the coming of a new generation, a wedding quilt is tangible consummation of a couple's love. Since pioneer days, women have stitched quilts as part of the dowry, to assure the bride and groom a life of warmth and closeness— and boding well wishes for their fertility.

Often, the patterns in a wedding quilt reflect the romance and intermingling of two lives—as in the interlocking rings of Double Wedding Ring, or the diamond bursts in Star of Bethlehem. Although these designs are characteristically for couples, the pattern is not what makes a wedding quilt, but rather the loving hands and blessings of family and friends that make it particularly sentimental.

# WEDDING BLESSINGS

*Perhaps the most intimate reason for quilts is to honor
the union of a man and a woman.*

# 31. DOUBLE WEDDING RING (74"x74")

Early in our marriage, Michael and I covered ourselves in the wedding quilt Michael had won as a teen, playing Bingo at Grandma Anna's church. Because Grandma made this special heirloom, we relished it on our bed for several months. But soon, as a young bride—and a new quilter—I wanted a wedding quilt from my own hands. This quilt would be particularly pretty and a gentle reminder of our vows to each other.

As I discovered being married was not easy, I chose a pattern that was similarly difficult. I knew that if I could overcome the challenges of double wedding ring, I could face the unknown trials of marriage. So I gathered scraps in my favorite light greens, and cut and pieced them lovingly together in a detailed, interlocking pattern.

As I stretched my quilt top proudly over the frame, my husband entered to announce his new job. We would be moving from our settled place in Pennsylvania to explore the mysteries of life in Michigan. The news sent my mind in all worried directions: Now I had to pack up my home; gather up our two baby daughters; and leave the loving embrace of Michael's family. What would life be like in this new place? How would I make friends? And would we belong?

Suitcases packed, and boxes stacked, I left the quilt on the frame up until our last few days in Pennsylvania. I didn't want to admit my life was changing. When Grandma Anna came to wish us well, she saw that I had still not completed my project. Anna gave me this word of advice: "Never pack an unfinished quilt." (I learned it rarely makes its way back to the frame.)

So Anna offered to take the quilt and finish it while we packed. I was touched by this woman's unconditional love: from taking us in when we needed a roof, to teaching me quilting when I needed an outlet—and now completing my quilt when I needed helping hands and comfort.

In just a few days, when our moving day had come, Anna appeared as we pulled out of the driveway, cradling what I thought was my finished quilt. But no: I noticed several dangling threads and fabric that looked like she had added a ruffle. To the contrary, she layered the top to the back, and sewed the binding to the quilt—but left the finishing to me! She even handed me a generous supply of precut thread and needles.

I didn't understand why she didn't finish my quilt, but soon learned that loose ends were her intent all along. In our nine hours' drive to Michigan, I hemmed and stitched, as my quilt consoled me and comforted my uneasy feelings about leaving. Finally when we arrived at this new and uncertain place, my quilt had become a source of strength, grounding me in hope, love, and even luck, and giving me confidence as we started our new journey.

Just as pioneers stacked everything on the wagon and headed to settle somewhere across the prairies, we had embarked on a similar journey, heading to start our life in Michigan. I realized I was no different than women 200 years before me, who made quilts not only to keep their family warm, but to warm their new home—and perhaps most importantly, to strengthen their spirits.

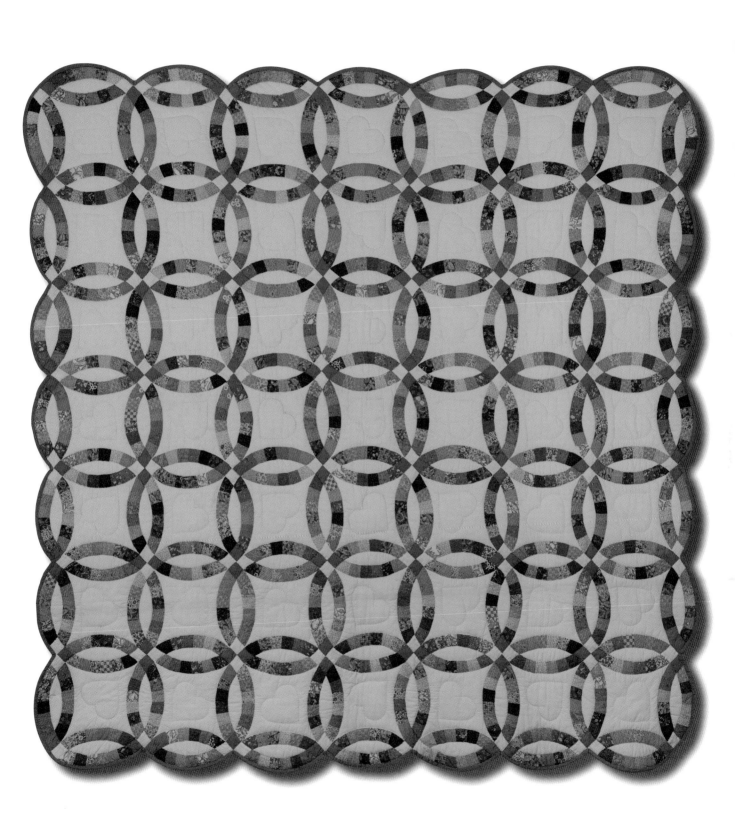

5th
Anniversary
1998

Anna
Sitar

Carol
Sitar

Edyta
Sitar

# 32. INDIAN WEDDING RING (75"x95")

Now approaching five years of marriage, I was learning the meaning of give and take—and that living with a man is more about giving. And so I wanted to give of my heart in a special five-year anniversary quilt.

Thanks to several years of quilting practice—and learning patience as a young wife and mother—I had gained the confidence to tackle more elaborate piecing and appliqué. So I added a touch of applique to this reverse wedding ring pattern. Multi-colored scraps establish a background for floating circles in crisp muslin.

I finished the top just in time, as we prepared for our annual family trip to celebrate Christmas in Pennsylvania. Proudly, I packed the quilt top to show Grandma Anna and my mother-in-law Carol. Of course, they wanted to see it immediately when we arrived. They promptly spread the quilt on the frame and we sat down to quilt my top together. We spent much of our time that holiday, chatting and stitching and sharing stories, while Delfina and Anna played with their presents. For us, this Christmas was a truly joyous time. I realized that marriage survives with support from the whole family, and that *quilting together is the ultimate gift.*

# 33. BETHLEHEM STAR (74"x74")

For the hundreds of heirlooms she made in her life, Grandma Anna considered every quilt precious. Imagine my surprise when I caught her cutting up a quilt and using a piece to dust her furniture! I later learned that Grandma had gently and lovingly pieced this "rag" as her wedding quilt 64 years ago. In her years of marriage, it had witnessed an almost full cycle of life: It blessed the birth of her three sons, mourned the loss of her husband, and offered comfort through tears and joy.

I was not only appalled that she was cutting the quilt, but eager to preserve the life it represented. Anna did not want to give me this cut-up remnant and instead, offered other meaningful treasures for me to keep, but I set my mind on saving this quilt.

I went home to salvage what pieces I could and reinvent the pattern for Sitar posterity. The result was this celebration of our 10-year anniversary—a Star of Bethlehem and variation of Grandma's wedding quilt. The explosion of color, starting from the center, speaks to my very humble beginnings and a family tradition that continues to grow, thanks to the quilting seeds that Anna planted.

## 34. ELDON (86"X86")

This quilt began as our 15-year anniversary tribute, but turned into a celebration of life and survival. While planning the pattern on my floor, I layered strips that became the foundation of eight-point stars, set into log cabins, grounded in black and brown centers. As I stitched the pieces together, I realized my quilting not only reflected my love of fabric and my love for Michael, but also my experience as a human being—how we grow and nourish each other in marriage, to become stronger, wiser, better people.

Then, I heard the story of a young man, Eldon, who inspired me in his determined fight against a life-threatening illness. At first, I began assembling this quilt as a material gift to mark our anniversary—but it became an object for recognizing Eldon's *superhuman* spirit at conquering his obstacles. I named this quilt in Eldon's honor, and he moved on to beat the odds.

The multi-layered meanings in Eldon's quilt teach that sometimes our best intentions unexpectedly turn to reveal a grander, more meaningful purpose.

## 35. CRAZY QUILT (70"x80")

As we approach 20 years of marriage, my wedding quilts have spanned our experience, reflecting the deepest love between us; our growing strength and synergy as a couple; our journey as parents; and our newest challenges as we approach middle age. Now I'm working on a *crazy quilt*. Enough said.

Strong women and men throughout our community are superheroes in their roles as leaders. Teaching by example, spending time, committing ideas, and investing their being, these leaders often perform thankless jobs. The album quilt offers a community means to acknowledge the contributions of their devoted friends and leaders.

Dating back to the 1830s, and popularized in Baltimore, Maryland, album quilts, or signature quilts, documented transient relationships, as American society moved westward. Consistent with an era of sentimentality, people looked to record their lives in poetry, music, and autograph books—and quilts became a form of fabric journaling.

Album quilts engaged a group of contributors, who would stitch and personalize an original square, often showcasing their creativity in embroidery and other embellishments. Whatever the design—whether pieced or appliquéd, a repeating quilt pattern, or individual blocks—a signed, stamped, or stitched signature typically marked the center, calling attention to the hand that made it.

# ALBUM QUILTS

*Album quilts offer heartfelt support from a group of people
to honor, thank, or recognize someone special.*

# 36. SIGNATURE QUILT (84"x86", IRREGULAR)

When I came upon this signature quilt, something about it made me want to hold onto it, to treasure the handwritten names upon the squares, and keep the work of these women alive. I looked closer to see more than 50 fading signatures, each representing someone, somewhere, in some community, who wanted to honor someone important.

All I know about the quilt is its age of approximately 200 years. I don't know any of the women who made it, nor the woman for whom they assembled it. But somehow, I feel a quilting connection that transcends our radically different worlds. Whatever the times or condition of society, the reason for quilts has remained a constant: to recognize people who touch our lives.

This signature quilt is one of a pair, which I purchased for posterity—in hopes that this "community" would stay together. Some makers signed their name in ink (as the medium was becoming more indelible); others owned a personalized stamp; and other more ambitious women wrote their name in thread. "Lucy" signed her name to this square.

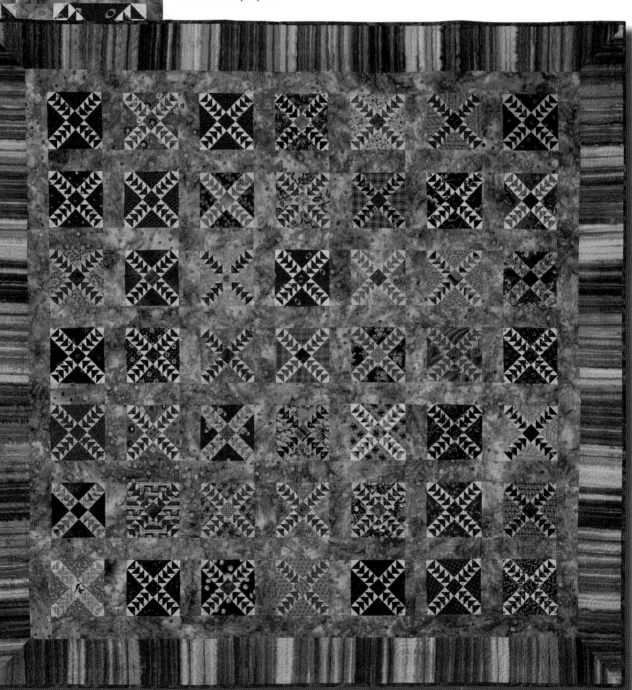

## 37. WINGS AND PRAYERS (68"x68")

A group of friends made most of the blocks for this signature quilt, with one variation: the signatures are missing. Each block follows the same Cross-Flying Geese pattern, and every one is made from different hands and different fabrics. We assembled and swapped the blocks in the weeks preceding Lent, stitching a square a day for each quilter in the group, and saying a prayer to wish her well.

Originating in New York State, this Cross-Flying Geese pattern is paper pieced and set on cross from point to point. Some squares are pieced in light and dark fabrics; others are blends of different fabrics that reflect the maker's personality. Tinted, hand-dyed, batik sashing and borders frame the squares from old and new friends—and although they do not bear any signatures, they create a blanket of heartfelt prayers.

# 38. A ROSE IS A ROSE (64"x64")

This Rose of Sharon pattern was the start of my exploration and fascination with Baltimore album quilts. This design repeats nine of the same blocks in three rows of three, finished with black triangles set on point, and fading into a dark black border. The pattern's simplicity and repetition contribute to this album quilt's appeal. The appliqué silhouettes are all the same, yet each has its own distinguishing characteristics.

## 39. ELEGANT GARDEN (52"x52")

A light muslin background is fertile ground for appliquéd flowers in bubble gum pinks, poison green, browns and cheddars. Just as in a bed of wildflowers, each of 24 blocks is a different bloom, nourished with fabrics, threads, and a quilter's green thumb. The flowers gather around a double eight-point star at the center, with edging reminiscent of a picket fence.

## 40. APPLIQUÉ AFFAIR (79"x79")

Following the thrill of planting my Elegant Garden (see
39. Elegant Garden, on the left page), my digression into
appliqué awakened my quilting spirit. Eager to explore, I
couldn't get enough of creating these dazzling dimensional
designs. Just thinking about the blooming possibilities,
I overstayed my welcome in my sewing room just so I
could fuss with the fabrics and shapes. What many quilters
consider a chore in needle turning, I saw as a pleasant,
moving experience. And when I wasn't sewing, I was
dreaming of designs that showed in my distant, starry eyes.

My family noticed my odd behavior, happier than usual,
constantly smiling, hardly eating, and disappearing. Finally
after days of enduring my demeanor, Michael accused me
of having an affair. Where had he gone wrong? And what
was I doing? He was right. I had been completely unfaithful
in ignoring him and indulging my fabric. In fact, I had an
appliqué affair!

# My Appliqué Affair...

## 41. SWEET SIXTEEN (76"x76")

Just as a young girl gains right of passage at her sweet sixteen, so I earned
passage into the art of appliqué with this Baltimore album design. Each of
sixteen, 16-inch blocks could be its own "coming out" party, celebrating the
fabric-on-fabric technique in cherry reds, moody blues, cheddar yellows,
and poison greens. A traditional red and Wedgwood blue floral border
complement the classic pattern.

Americans are proud of their democracy, their visionary leaders, and personal freedoms. When our nation celebrates, we rejoice. When it mourns, we cry. And when it honors, we respect. As the world becomes increasingly global, we learn to more deeply understand our place in it. Quilts help express our social experience as part of a larger, unified cause that values vision, equality, and opportunity.

# SOCIAL STATEMENTS

*Quilts document relevant historical happenings that reach beyond
the personal sphere to touch a community, state, or even nation.*

## 42. 9-11 (80"x92")

I sat stunned, along with millions of other people, as New York's Twin Towers crumbled into dust—not because of some natural disaster, but because of some unthinkable, horrific human act. As if penetrating each of our deepest souls, the 9-11 tragedy changed lives, and I was among the awestruck and angered. With my children by my side, I was frozen in motion, not knowing how to respond or retaliate. At the same time, my husband was flying for a business trip, and I could not settle my racing thoughts: Where was he now? What should I do? Where were all the other spouses of the people caught in this unexplainable crossfire?

So I started cutting pieces and more pieces of fabric, inspired by the New York Beauty pattern. Reminded of the Statue of Liberty's crown, I gripped the scissors as if clutching my freedom. I hoped that by piecing the fabrics back together, I could repair the damage this catastrophe had caused. The colors and shapes reflect my inner explosion and the lasting effects in the days and months that followed.

In fact, this quilt took nearly a half-year to finish, as I machine pieced and then hand quilted the layers. The truth is I probably would have finished sooner, but perhaps in its making, I was also healing. On that somber September 11th day, we all felt as if we lost control, and in some small way, quilting helped me regain it.

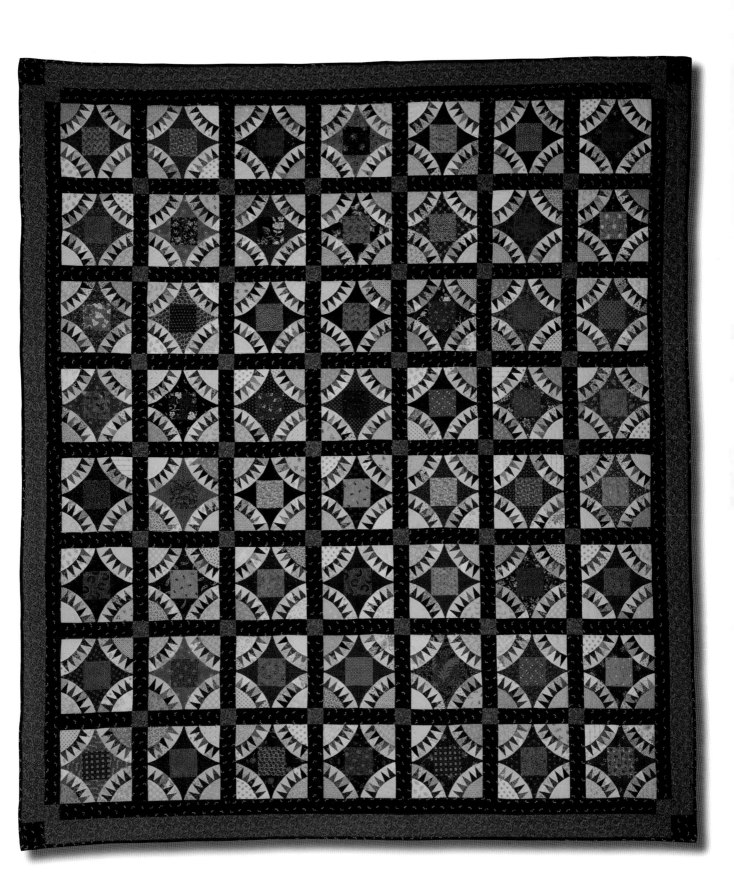

## 43. BICENTENNIAL (88"x92")

When the United States of America marked 200 years of existence, Michael's Grandma Anna Sitar celebrated, too. In this classic 1970s quilt—made in honor of the Bicentennial—Anna stitched an icon of her times. Following her recycling instincts—and likely with few other fabric resources—she started with a white bed sheet and leftover scraps of Sunday suits she had sewn from the period's most popular fabrics: red and blue polyester. (How she succeeded at appliquéing such stretchy fabric is still a mystery, but somehow Anna got it to behave.)

As with all of her other quilts, Anna made this one to hang in the church. She appliquéd flags, embroidered stars, and added an eagle with open wings. After hand quilting, she finished the edges with a red ruffle, typical of quilts made during this time. But one question remained: Where did she find enough leftover scraps to make such a long, dramatic border? She looked at me with her serious eyes and admitted she did not use scraps. To finish her project, she tapped into special resources. She had cut up her skirt to make the ruffle!

Anna continued teaching me life lessons: Women of the 70s were domestic queens. Certainly they were housewives in every respect, but they also represented pillars of the family: If scraps wouldn't do, they found other means to satisfy their creative ends. In this case, a quilt for her church and her community was more important than a skirt for herself.

# 44. AMERICAN BEAUTY (80"x92")

US citizenship is among the world's most coveted prizes, as it recognizes our nation of individuals, who together embrace a system of core beliefs: in choice, tolerance, equality, justice, and hope in the idea that anything is possible.

A group of friends made the blocks for this quilt to celebrate my belonging in America. Now I had found a life and a home—but most importantly, I found my identity. As I assembled the blocks to document this important milestone, I was keenly aware of our blessings in being here and participating in a country of immeasurable opportunities.

*In the centers of some blocks, my friends included fabrics that symbolize the things they wish for me. The Lady of Liberty, shown here, is a powerful reminder of where I've been and how far I've come—to a place that permits my unbounded expression and fulfillment in sharing quilts with the world.*

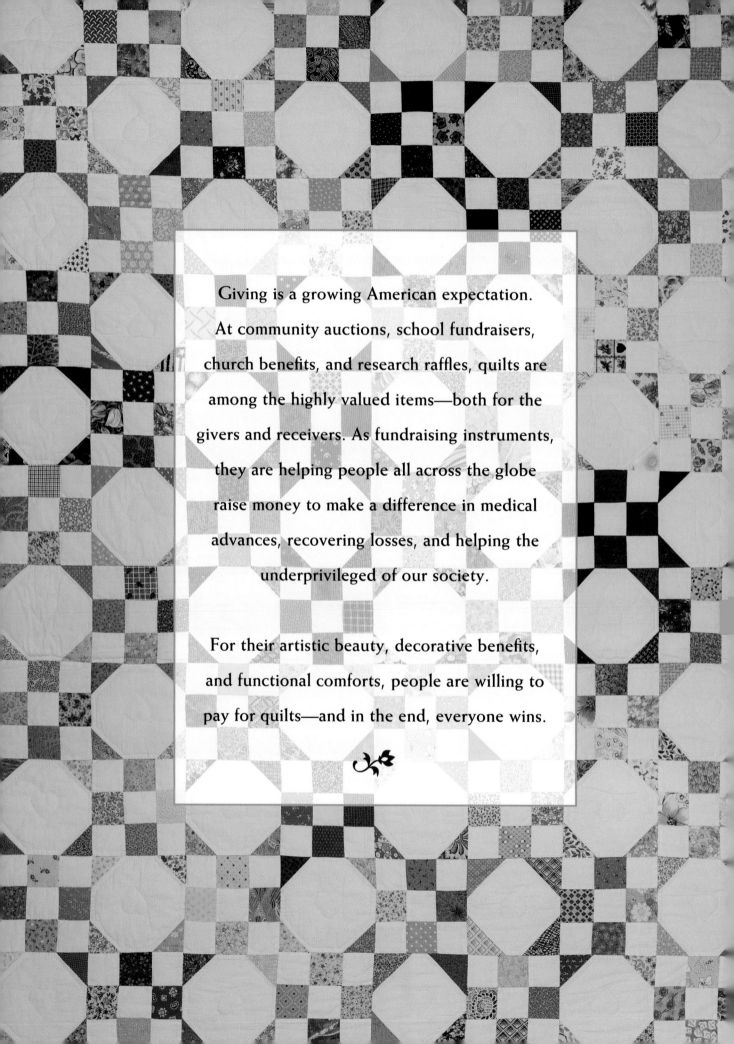

Giving is a growing American expectation. At community auctions, school fundraisers, church benefits, and research raffles, quilts are among the highly valued items—both for the givers and receivers. As fundraising instruments, they are helping people all across the globe raise money to make a difference in medical advances, recovering losses, and helping the underprivileged of our society.

For their artistic beauty, decorative benefits, and functional comforts, people are willing to pay for quilts—and in the end, everyone wins.

# CREATING VALUE

Quilts represent value in our society,
as cherished prizes at benefits and fundraisers.

## 45. MILLENNIUM QUILT (84"X108")

As our family settled in southern Michigan, the Calico Quilters Guild in Battle Creek welcomed me enthusiastically. For several years, I quilted with these women, not only finding an outlet for my stitching, but also connecting with a warm circle of friends. Then in 2000, with news of my husband's new job, we learned we would be moving away from the area. I mourned my distance from these spirited women and wished I could stay in this happy place.

At the same time, the Calico Quilters were hosting a fundraising event; and of course, I wanted to support the effort. Raffle tickets were one dollar each, or six for five dollars. As my group anticipated my departure, and given the last-minute notice, they surely wouldn't have time to make me a farewell quilt. So my friends encouraged me to stock up on raffle tickets. If I couldn't leave with a custom quilt, at least I would leave with a quilt from their hands.

As luck would have it that prophetic evening, I won the raffle—and the prize was this sentimental quilt to which every Calico Quilter contributed. Donating fabric, piecing and stitching the blocks, appliquéing the border, and hand quilting the layers, my buddies had unknowingly made me a blanket steeped in their caring and compassion. As I began a new chapter in my life—reluctant to leave these people behind—I was lucky to take a piece of them with me in this meaningful and heartfelt souvenir.

Mere mention of the word holidays stirs up
emotions, often connected to faith and family.
From religious events to hard-earned vacation
time, holidays are meant for celebrating
togetherness. Quilters anticipate and reflect
on these times by stitching colors and images
of the season into their quilts for decorating
and giving. They also seek out souvenir fabrics
from quilt shops in the cities and towns they
visit, giving them added destination spots and
keepsakes they can preserve in their quilts.

In realizing the wonder of the calendar's
rhythms, in travel, and even unforgettable
foods, quilts help us recall our family rituals,
and nostalgically, relive the feelings.

# HOLIDAYS AND RITUAL EVENTS

As relaxation or religious ceremony, holidays mark memorable life occasions,
which lend themselves to the making of quilts.

## 46. ALOHA (55"x55")

Like a "fabric postcard" that documents our travels, this quilt captures my family's dreamy time in the Hawaiian Islands. Inspired by the rainforest's tropical landscape, sensual light rains, and exotic blooms, I wanted to transplant the paradise in fabric. The resulting collection of pineapple greens, sunshine yellows, and ocean blues adds a glow to this Hawaiian appliqué. Just as traveling broadens our perspectives, the design begins at the center and branches into four directions. Three shades offer a subtle twist to traditional two-color Hawaiian appliqué.

# 47. TROPICAL TURNOVERS (62"x62")

As we toured the lush Hawaiian Islands, the tropical influence permeated everywhere. Juicy, ripe pineapple, meaty mangoes, and creamy coconut—all as if freshly picked from the trees—transformed our meals into exotic elegance. Each morning of our visit, irresistible pastries enticed me to sample all the flavors. Warm, buttery crust on the outside, and delicately balanced tropical fruit on the inside, woke up my tastes in a gourmet luau.

Perhaps it was the fact that we were dining in Hawaii—or that I was loving the face time with my family—but these turnovers had such power over me, I had to capture their taste in a quilt. Here, scraps of batiks in multi-colors reflect Hawaii's tropical fruits and flowers, and awaken my taste for these sinful turnovers…almost as if fresh from the oven.

## 48. SNOWFLAKE (68"x68")

Ask most Midwesterners about the snow, and they'll tell you winters are long and dreary. In my spirit of finding good and enjoying nature's gifts, I look forward to the season's first flurries. Because I am an avid gardener, I surrender to the sun, planting, weeding, and massaging the soil. When winter finally arrives, the weather lets me off the hook. Now I can stay inside for my quiet time, without that "garden guilt."

For me, the snow is a welcome sign that equates to creative time. On this particular wintry day, I sat in my living room, pondering the colors of the winter sky. This boundless canvas of blue and gray—and every shade along the spectrum—began delivering its white fragile flecks, floating, drifting, and happily riding the currents in the air. I hurried to the door to catch the scene, hoping the flakes would linger longer.

I tried to capture that fleeting feeling in fabric, recreating those heavenly blues and whites, the first two colors in my "Let It Snow" fabric line. In this quilt, snowflakes are set on point with light sashing in between.

## 49. MIDNIGHT BLOOM (53"x53")

I relish the moments the morning after a snow, when that white wintry blanket is still fresh and untouched, reflecting nature's gentle side. Imagining the trees budding secretly while we sleep, I created this quilt of midnight blooms. The branches are appliquéd in browns and greens, while buds show delight in cheddar and blue.

But the purity soon gives way to snowplows, car exhaust, and messy tracks, turning the innocence to dirty gray, the third color in the "Let It Snow" fabric collection, shown here on the border of the quilt.

## 50. WINTER LILIES (57"x57")

Whatever their faith or seasonal rituals, people find common ground in snowflakes and neutral winter quilts like this one. In navy blue and off-white appliqué (made from the same fabrics in the previous two quilts), these lily baskets decorate for any winter holiday—*or no holiday at all.*

As if frozen in full bloom, nine lily baskets and a border of appliquéd branches reflect the wishful gardener in me, as I anticipate return of warmer weather. The frosty white images remind me of my childhood, as I finger-painted pictures on our frozen windows.

# 51. BELIEVE (63"x63")

Just as some of us wear our hearts on our sleeves, we stitch our feelings into quilts through fabric, color, and pattern choices. This quilt expresses these feelings upfront in a pattern called "Frosty Window." As if looking through the window of a home at the holidays—observing traditions of feasting, giving, sharing, and rejoicing—the words on the fabric make us want to partake.

*In family, friends, peace, and hope,* the words evoke much deeper emotions that urge us to set our differences aside, rebuild our ties, and discover the holidays' true gifts.

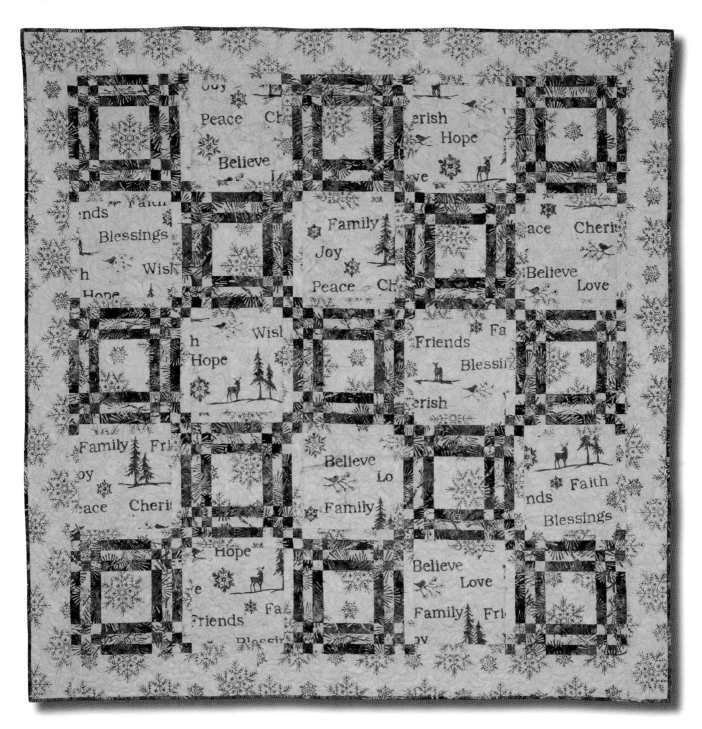

# 52. CHRISTMAS JOY (82"x81")

As we repeat holiday rituals of entertaining friends, baking sweets, and nostalgically decorating, we try to recapture that part of Christmas: the feeling of being a child again. With our innocent wishes and unbridled excitement, we dream of presents that take us back in time. No matter what our age, we still find delight in imagining the surprises Santa has delivered.

This year, our tree was especially glowing. After the children had opened their gifts, we were basking in the Christmas morning moments, when I noticed one box remained unopened with my name on it. Signed, "Love, Michael," this gift was clearly not the usual socks or kitchen appliance that we housewives "earned." It was not my annual flannel nightgown, but a box of something I didn't expect: a quilter's wish in an antique quilt!

As if I were four years old again—having dreamed and dreamed of my favorite dolly—now excitement rushed through my veins as I opened the folds of this precious heirloom. So old and fragile—and yet so spirited—this wise piece of art had stirred my senses.

This quilt was my Christmas wish-come-true—and now every year, I recreate those feelings, gently unfolding my quilt under the tree after all the gifts are gone. I wrap it around the base like a tree skirt around a beautiful girl. Every year I unveil my quilt, I am mesmerized again and again, as if seeing it for the very first time. The exquisite pieces—¾-inch squares and small triangles—come together in remarkable, unconventional patterns, each with a cheddar-yellow center that somehow bears hope for a coming year of peace.

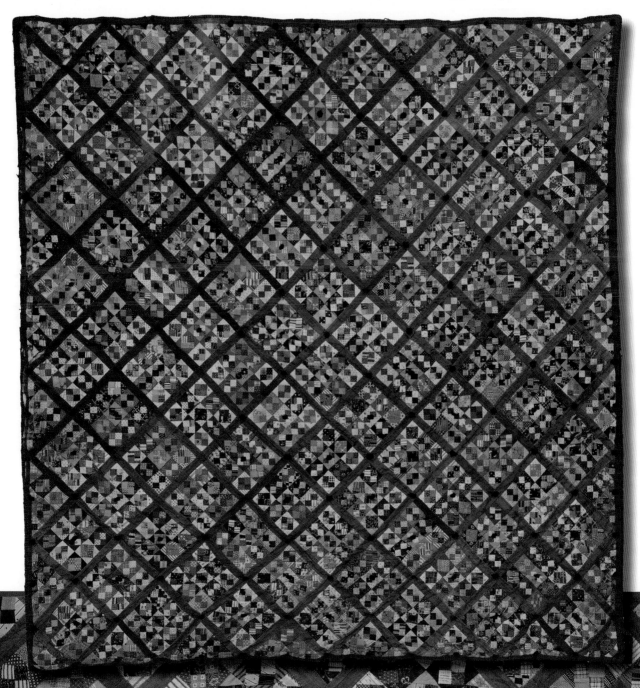

# 53. VALENTINE'S GOODIES (69"x73")

Michael learned quickly how to woo me with gifts of stunning antique quilts. On Valentine's Day, I came upon a box unpretentiously wrapped on our kitchen table. This was not a customary bunch of flowers, nor was it a store-bought box of chocolate candies, but some would argue it was better than bonbons. This antique quilt was filled with surprises that made me want to indulge in every square.

Each block is a different pattern and dimension, beginning with cross-flying geese at the center, reminiscent of lemon jellies dipped in sugar. Some red and brown squares like chocolate cherries, others yellow and cream like coconut and almonds, this Valentine's gift is a gourmet sampler.

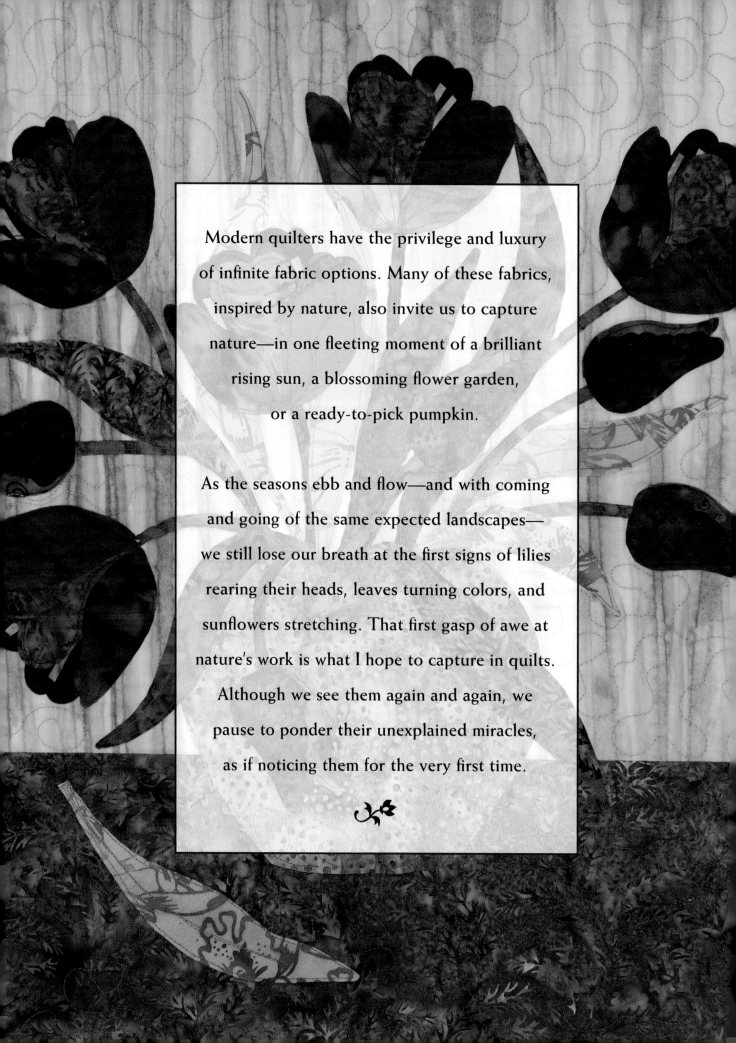

Modern quilters have the privilege and luxury
of infinite fabric options. Many of these fabrics,
inspired by nature, also invite us to capture
nature—in one fleeting moment of a brilliant
rising sun, a blossoming flower garden,
or a ready-to-pick pumpkin.

As the seasons ebb and flow—and with coming
and going of the same expected landscapes—
we still lose our breath at the first signs of lilies
rearing their heads, leaves turning colors, and
sunflowers stretching. That first gasp of awe at
nature's work is what I hope to capture in quilts.
Although we see them again and again, we
pause to ponder their unexplained miracles,
as if noticing them for the very first time.

# SEASON'S BEAUTY

*In their captivating colors, sensual textures, and stunning imagery,*
*quilts express our awe of the natural world.*

## 54. POPPIES (20"X24")

As a young girl, my fascination with flora and fauna led me to pause at the roadside poppies. Maybe it was their passionate red or the watchful black eye at the center of their blooms that attracted my childhood curiosity. Or perhaps I related to poppies' wild instincts in blanketing the floor of the woods. In any case, these tiny coins stirred me to recreate them in fabric.

This was the first quilt I made with raw-edge appliqué, where shapes are stitched to the anchor fabric without turning the edges under. The technique enabled me to echo nature in its unfinished edges and striking shapes and colors.

Eager to perfect my hand at raw-edge appliqué and to continue practicing "fabric painting,"
## I quilted a garden of other blooms...

### 55. TIGER LILIES (22"x25")

Symbols of wealth and prosperity, these bursts of orange and purple blooms signify the coming of spring. Batik fabrics imitate flower petals in their variegated colors and textures.

### 56. IRIS (20"x24")

Iris means *rainbow*, as it blooms in a spectrum of vibrant colors. Some people believe the flowers symbolize eloquence—fitting for these showy purple varieties.

### 57. SUNFLOWER (20"x24")

As if smiling on summer's brilliance, luminous yellow faces bring sunshine indoors.

## 58. TULIPS (20"x22")

Like goblets that hold the secrets to life, these colorful signs of spring reach full bloom in fabric.

## 59. OVER THE FENCE (20"x18")

Black-eyed Susans flourish along a roadside picket fence, a familiar scene for this common American wildflower.

## 60. GERANIUMS (20"x22")

Perched in a pot on a windowsill, hearty geraniums admire the sky outside. Patterned green fabrics reflect the plant's characteristic curly leaves.

## 61. CLEMATIS
(12"x40" Table Runner)

As if climbing wildly up a trellis, clematis wander freely across a table runner.

## 62. LOCATION, LOCATION, LOCATION (36"x51")

Just as human beings seek out the perfect home, so do birds build the perfect place to nest. This scene is from a place in my backyard, where wildlife coexists in peace, and weeds live in harmony with flowers.

## 63. HOLDING ON (32"x21")

As greens of summer begin to fade, we feel the onset of autumn's orange. Recalling lazy days in the shade, carefree strolls, running bases, mowing lawns, and restless robins, we want to hold on to sunny weather. Similarly, as we grow through life—lose our leaves and face our changes—we must muster the strength simply to hold on; to preserve our memories of happy occasions; and know that even through stormy weather, another season will come to pass.

## 64. FALL MEMORIES (34"x26")

I remember fondly my walks in the woods, as I held my mother's hand and breathed deeply to inhale the earthy aroma of the trees around me. Walks were the highlights of my childhood, giving me "alone time" with my mom and my greatest pleasure in gathering leaf bouquets. Though my mother probably wanted to tire me out, I never tired of our time in the forest.

Once home, my mother would gather up my leaves and display them proudly on our dining room table, as if arranging a wedding centerpiece. Fussing and finding the right vase to hold them, she treasured this bunch of curling flora, knowing full well it wouldn't last beyond a day—but giving us reason to replenish the bunch with another walk together in the woods.

## 65. HARVEST PUMPKINS (38"x28")

Of all the seasons, I relish autumn for its rustic shades of red, yellow, and orange. Feeding our instincts for hunting and gathering, fall is a time to celebrate the harvest, in picking pumpkins, raking leaves, and taking stock of our ever-changing lives.

Stemming back to pioneer days, quilts have
played multiple roles in the home, not only as
functional blankets for keeping warm at night,
but for adding color to rooms, decorating beds
and walls, and even blocking breezes
in the days before sliding doors.

Just as birds flit resolutely to build their nests
of twigs, women stitch ceremoniously to
personalize their homes with quilts.

# NESTING INSTINCTS

*From bed covers to table runners that rotate with the seasons,
quilts in the home serve deliberate purpose—yet they always embody
a woman's nurturing instincts to love and care for her family.*

# 66. ROCKING CHAIR QUILT (83"x72")

This antique quilt is peaceful and soothing in its thousands of muted, colorful pieces. In some magical way, it has calmed my family through physical and emotional ups and downs. It still holds its dignified place on the chair that rocked me and Michael, and our three little babies through countless helpless, wakeful nights.

As they grew, whenever my children cried, they reached for this quilt. When they felt alone, they found friendship in it. And whenever they felt under the weather, this quilt has been their healing embrace. Cradling, caressing, and swaddling us as one, this quilt supplanted our growing pains with reassurance that we would be all right.

Its value shows in the gently chewed corners; the matted batting where little fingers have traced lines; and tattered edges that clearly have been touched—over and over again. No matter how weathered the pieces become, this quilt will always reaffirm our connections. Between husband and wife, parent and child, and perhaps some day, in grown child and aging parent, this quilt is witness to our vulnerabilities and yet, remains our source of strength.

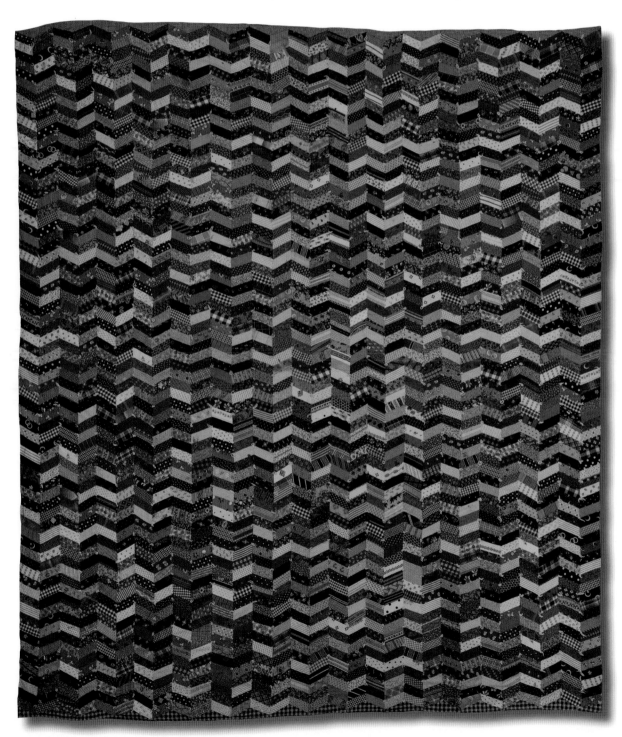

## 67. MOUNTAIN TOP (88"x74")

The most common utilitarian quilts are made for beds, which is where this story begins. I wanted to create a quilt large enough to cover a queen-size bed. I turned to a bottomless bag of half-square triangles I had collected in an exchange with my friends—and now I was ready to make the climb. In this 30-block quilt, I assembled 720 triangles—24 triangles per block—tied together with same-color triangles, which framed the quilt in an ascending mountain design.

When my friends all saw the finished results, they wanted to try making this same quilt for themselves. Like an avalanche, the enthusiasm gathered momentum among the group, and they all began climbing to the same Mountain Top. What began as a personal quilting challenge became a thrilling journey for our group— and a new collection of quilted beauties for our beds.

## 68. BROKEN HANDLE (79"x66")

In my search for a cover for our guest room bed, I came across this antique, unfinished quilt top. With its blue and pink baskets and green filler blocks, it was the perfect happy pattern to welcome overnight visitors. Yet the baskets were missing handles… maybe the maker avoided appliqué!

In any case, the pattern's simple, original design was certainly suitable for my guests. So I added a pink binding for a feminine finish. Now the orphaned top has found its home on our guest bed and sometimes on an empty wall. If I squint my eyes, I see hearts in the baskets, reassuring me *this quilt was made with love.*

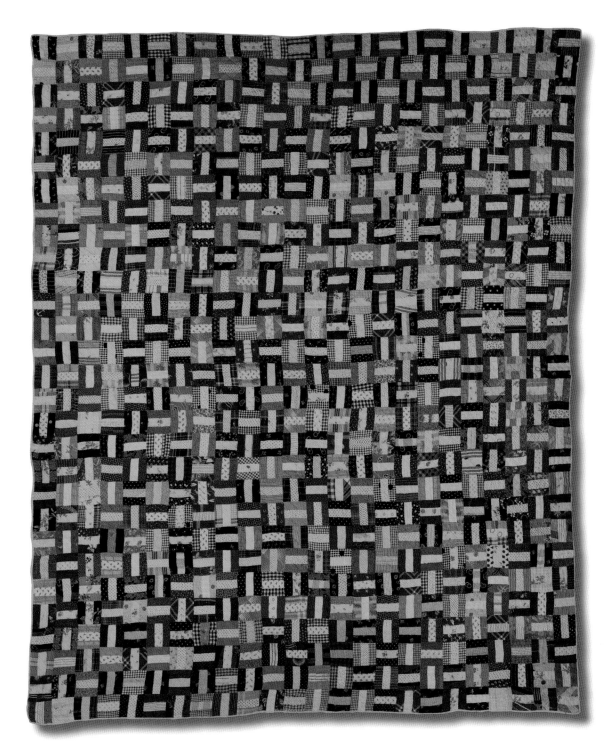

## 69. RECYCLED BEAUTY (83"x67")

This antique quilt captures a bygone era, when women relied on old, worn-out clothes for fabric to make their quilts. Remnants of men's shirts and pants, and women's skirts and blouses came together in striking strips, as in this randomly pieced example. Light fabrics interlaced between darks create a braided, dimensional look.

When Michael gave me this souvenir quilt from his travels, at first, I cooed at its scrappy, weathered charm, but also noticed its unusual construction. At first, I disregarded its thicker, heavier weight, but soon my curiosity consumed me.

I had to see what secrets lie inside. As I gently unraveled the worn seams, I pulled back the fabric to reveal hidden layers: There inside this beautiful antique quilt was a second tattered quilt, sandwiched between the wool!

While desperately preserving the outside quilted layers, I felt compelled to unveil this inner secret: a pink and mint green triangle treasure. Though the quilt had seen better days, it was clear someone wanted to keep it and love it—and what better way to recycle the warmth than to layer it into another quilt?

107

# 70. DRESDEN STAR (66"x50")

Quilts are destined not only for the bed, but also for tables, walls, and other furnishings. This quilt captures both past and present, starting with Dresden Plate, a popular Depression era pattern. I added glow to the vintage design by folding light-colored triangles in half and setting them into the seam. When opened, they created additional points that burst into a circle. Soft blue sashing with beet-red-and-blue-striped border frame this quilt to draw attention on any wall.

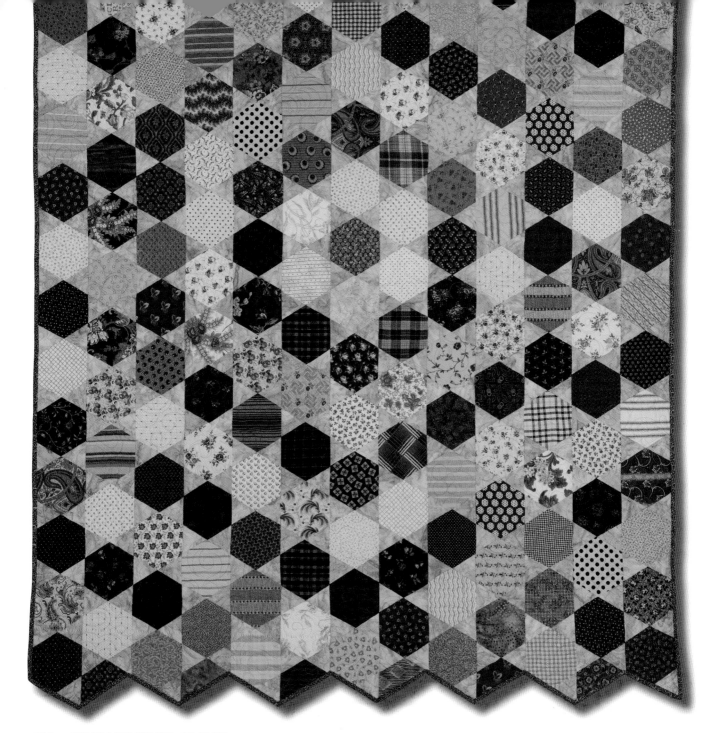

# 71. SUNSHINE BOX (64"x49")

As much as we try to see the good in the world, life delivers us samplings of bad. At this particular point in my adulthood, I found myself feeling sad and empty, as if the sun had set on my days. When my dearest friends, Chris and Michael, heard news of my distress—and despite my wishes not to come—they and their five children rushed to my door from Shipshewana, Indiana, bearing boxes and big smiles.

"We are bringing sun into your life," they explained, handing me a box filled with dozens of wrapped gifts. Whether a jar of homemade strawberry jam, a box of tea and honey, or a colorful scarf, the gifts were meant to replace my sadness with joy—and blessings from Chris and Michael's whole Amish community. In the Amish tradition, this "sunshine box"

brings rays of light whenever one feels sad, no matter what the circumstance. "Open a gift whenever you need it," they advised. Their gesture touched me so tenderly and deeply, it inspired the making of this quilt.

Hexagons and 60° yellow triangles are set in a trip-around-the-world pattern to show that eventually, happiness does come around, and that despite bad times, we can find small rays of light. The sunshine box changed my perspective: It was not the material gifts that comforted me, but the heartfelt kindness that wrapped each one. The box reminded me of my very special friends, who supported me in prayer and spirit. This simple token of caring and compassion would help me overcome these difficult times.

# 72. KALEIDOSCOPE (52"x52")

As a young girl, I was always bothered by cold things on my skin. Whenever I sat at the table or in an armchair, I preferred soft textures to cushion my arms and legs. (Or maybe I tell myself this story as an excuse for making another quilt.) I had already covered the beds and the walls with quilts, and now I was moving on to tabletops and dressers.

This quilt recaptures my childhood fascination with kaleidoscopes, those rotating telescopic toys that reveal ever-changing patterns and colors. Here, strips of Civil War reproduction fabrics join with other scraps in a four-pointed star, set on a dreamy blue background.

Busy patterns like these play well into table decorations, as they brighten up dining space, even in the dead of winter. A simple bouquet of bland, brown branches finds its "flowers" in the quilt beneath it, allowing us to dream of summer blooms long before the season arrives.

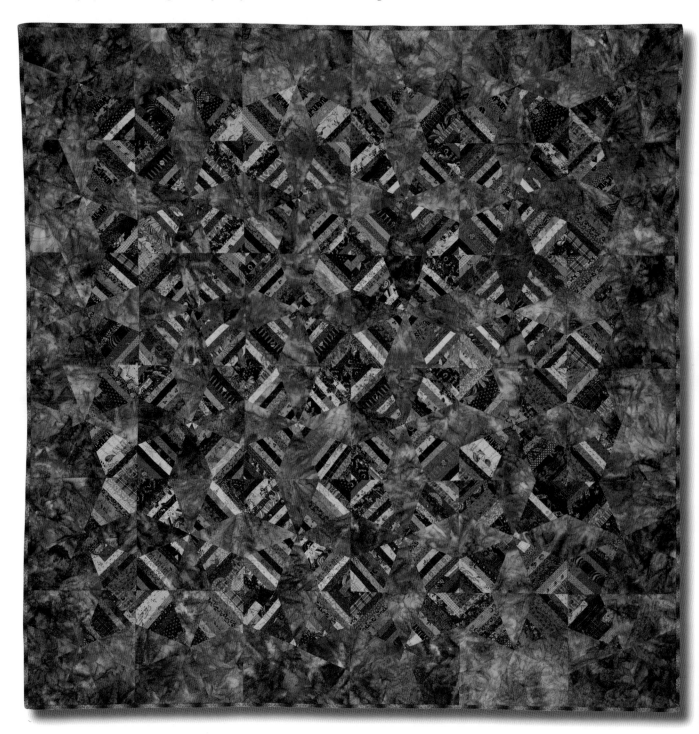

## 73. DOUBLE DARE (53"x53")

My friends had come to know me as the "scrappy quilter," utilizing all the colors of the rainbow and improbable fabric combinations. With this quilt, I wanted to challenge my instincts and limit my piecing to only two colors: black and yellow. I started with black stars and yellow filler blocks, but couldn't control my bend to blend. I came to realize I see the world in color—and admit that two tones are not enough for me.

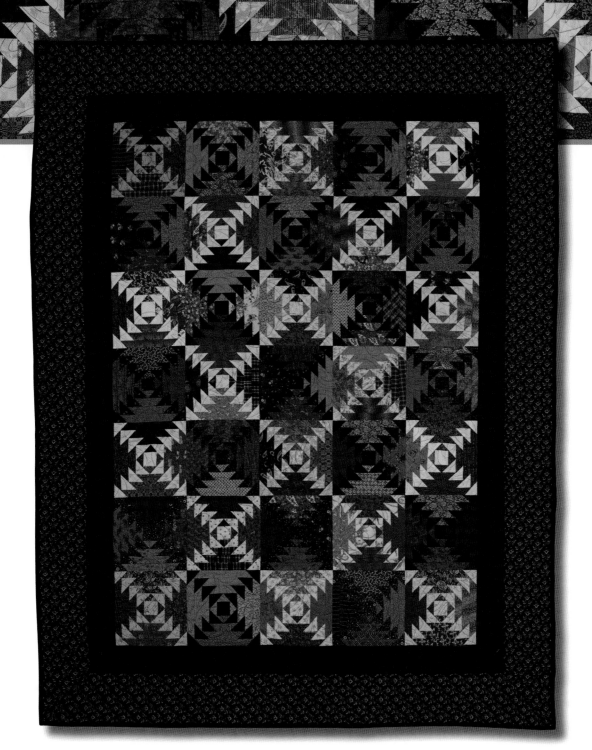

# 74. ON EAGLE'S WINGS (51"x66")

After Grandma Anna had fought cancer three times, it came time for her to surrender. This is the last quilt she held in her hands before she passed away. Looking at me with those penetrating eyes, this time her gaze was one of approval, visibly proud of my place in the family tree, and of passing her quilting legacy on to me.

As I watched her finger the paper-pieced pineapples and trace the lines of the flying geese, I felt as if I was flying with her. Grandma had given me wings in showing me the art and tradition of quilting—and in giving me the freedom to express myself. I learned not only how to rock the needle, but also to find life and joy in these woven fibers.

With Grandma's gentle hand and guidance, quilting had made me a better person. She taught me to create and not destroy; that we make quilts from love, not hate; and through them, teach lessons of warmth and giving, comfort and joy.

I named this quilt "On Eagle's Wings," for the song we sang, as we carried Grandma Anna through her beloved church. From her countless Bingo auction quilts to the Bicentennial Quilt that hung from the rafters of this very sanctuary, Grandma Anna had given her talent to the church—and now it was time for me to carry on.

Quilts are like songs. One person starts
singing, and others sing along, interpreting the
patterns for themselves, rejoicing in the infinite
variations, and finding meaning in their own
and others' creations. The quilts in this chapter
remind us to continue learning, to laugh every
day, and play as if we are children again. No
matter how old we become in years, we can
consciously keep our spirits young by living
(and quilting) in the moment.

Mindful of the child in me, I love to please,
to push the limits, and surround myself with
happy people—and teaching about quilts makes
me smile all the time. Whether showing a new
technique, demonstrating color combinations, or
continuing a closely held family tradition, these
quilts are meant to light a spark and make quilts
accessible to any willing hands.

Remembering Grandma Anna's gentle teaching,
these quilts give back what she gave me:
freedom to experiment with fabrics and colors,
techniques that speak to our busy lives, and
personal pride in every stitch. These are the
simplest reasons for making quilts:
*simply to have fun.*

# INSPIRING OTHERS

*We make quilts to unleash our passion on the world,
to share, teach, and learn from each other.*

## 75. SHOOTING STAR (70"x70")

With this quilt, I wanted to break the rules. Old traditions meet new techniques in this Shooting Star variation. I modernized a vintage, hand-stitched design by setting in folded fabrics, resulting in sharp points and flourishing bursts of color.

This quilt proves disparate fabrics can finally play together! Yes, batiks can live peaceably alongside prints. Here, setting floral triangles melt into a batik border. This "revelation" marks a turning point in my fabric designing, as before I designed in only batiks. Now I let myself off the hook to mix and match whatever patterns come to mind. This quilt's lesson: It's okay to be different.

## 76. DREAMING (70"x70")

Friends often want to know if I ever sleep at night: Where do I find my inspiration? When I lay my head on the pillow at night, I close my eyes and colors come pouring, as if freeing my imagination. Dreaming in rainbows is surely a gift, as ideas for me are constantly flowing, filling books of scribbles and sketches, waiting for me to make them real.

This quilt captures my mind's kaleidoscope, using fabrics exclusively from one of my favorite collections, Dreaming in Color. The many layers of shapes and patterns convey the constant dialog in my head and illustrate the colorful show we can create, simply by "forgetting" to follow the rules.

## 77. MARYANN (74"x74")

Teaching quilting is my passion—and often, my only reason for quilt making. Sometimes in the process of teaching others, I find my students teach me in return. This quilt is named for a special student, who taught me that quilting is a universal language. In a class of 27 other women, Maryann looked at me intently, yet with a noticeably empty stare. I wondered if perhaps she was scared to stitch, or if she was afraid to ask—but then I realized she didn't understand. Maryann and I spoke very different languages, but for her, the barrier was not an obstacle. She wanted to quilt, and I was there to teach her.

Quickly establishing our mutual goals—for Maryann to learn and me to show her how—the two of us focused our hands on creating. With very few words and lots of gestures, I modeled, pointed, smiled, and guided her along every quilt-making step. And she followed closely to accomplish her project, just as splendidly as any other student. In the end, I realized teaching quilting is much more than showing how to cut and stitch; it's for bringing people to new understanding, no matter what language they speak.

# 78. SUNSET (80"x64")

Besides sharing techniques and ideas through guilds and workshops, printed patterns reach quilters beyond the classroom. In mapping the puzzles, numbers, and pieces, patterns extend the teaching challenge, and enable others to find joy in quilting, even when they can't be learning face-to-face. When a simple photo on the front of a pattern inspires a quilter to make an heirloom, that quilting pattern has done its job.

# 79. FEATHERED STAR (73"x73")

Quilts also demonstrate new, inventive fabric combinations. This quilt uses fabrics I designed in unexpected ways. Where many quilts relegate large prints to the border, here the florals are the center of attention. Olive green, half-square triangle stars frame each spray of variegated blooms, and vintage blue diamonds guide the eye to the edge.

## 80. SUMMER STAR (68"x68")

Designing a fabric line is like raising 40 children. You want to give every fabric equal attention, and allow them the freedom to grow and explore. For every line I create, I build a quilt "family" of several patterns: one quilt of several select fabrics, another that uses all the fabrics, and a final quilt that uses alternative combinations. The grouping shows that just as we raise our children to be individuals, each fabric has a voice and a purpose for being. This quilt is the signature piece that uses all of the fabrics from my Sweet Sixteen collection.

## 81. MICHIGAN CROSSROADS (63"x70")

Patterns in the pages of books and magazines inspire not only avid quilters, but also those who dream of quilting. Because these resources enjoy a lasting shelf life, quilters often pass them among each other, spreading quilting culture even deeper. Some of my quilts, like this one, have been published in magazines, offering options for different colors, and showing readers the path to quilting. I named it Michigan Crossroads in honor of the opportunities my Midwest life has allowed. Now in making this pattern public, I can share the thrill with other quilters.

# 82. REACHING OUT (68"x74")

Grandma Anna planted a quilting seed in me—and I have nurtured it to flourish. This quilt represents my personal journey, as three rows of appliqué wind upwards and outwards. The design reflects my family's influence, incorporating nine-patches made by my mother, and reflecting Grandma Anna's sturdy roots.

While this chapter ends,
quilting continues. Even
though we may not notice,
reasons for quilts will
always exist—driving us
to piece just one more top,
to celebrate our joys and
release our inhibitions.
Or perhaps, we quilt for
the sake of our stash,
simply because we love our
fabric and the lasting lore
that quilts provide.

# INDEX OF QUILTS

For patterns to make many of the quilts featured in this book, visit www.laundrybasketquilts.com.
Other quilts are from the Sitar Family Collection, for which patterns are not available.

## RESOURCES

Laundry Basket Quilts ......................... www.laundrybasketquilts.com
Moda Fabrics .................................................... www.unitednotions.com
Landauer Corporation ................................... www.landauercorp.com

Accomplish Quilting ..................... www.accomplishquilting.com
Aurifil™ Threads.................................................... www.aurifil.com
Quilting Creations International.............. www.quiltingcreations.com

Judith Stern Friedman ............................................jsfcom@ameritech.net
Hardy Design Studio ............................www.hardydesignstudio.com

# Threading the Needles...

## Meet Edyta Sitar

Edyta's lifelong relationship with fabric began in Poland at a very young age, when she cut her mother's drapes to design her first project. Fortunately, for all of us, Edyta's mother recognized her passion for fabric that would later unfold into a consummate gift.

One of Edyta's dearest blessings is her marriage to her husband, Michael—and connection to the Sitar family quilting tradition. Both her mother-in-law, Carol, and grandmother-in-law, Anna, sat with Edyta over the quilt frame to teach her the ins and outs of quilting—and the ups and downs of life. With the help of two generations of Sitar women, Edyta found her confidence in this cottage craft, not only as a boundless creative outlet, but also as a means to filter her passion.

In observing the beauty of things around her, experiencing the thrills and challenges of being a woman, and reflecting deeply on the human condition, Edyta expresses her existence through quilts. "My children and my husband are my greatest motivation," she says. "This is a Cinderella dream for me. Being able to do what I love and share this love with others is the greatest feeling and reward I could imagine!"

Edyta's intuitive feel for fabric, keen eye for color, and family teachings all contribute to her amazing quilts and natural evolution to pattern and fabric designing. Now working as owner and co-founder of Laundry Basket Quilts (www.laundrybasketquilts.com), Edyta has created close to 150 quilt patterns, traditional and batik fabrics with Moda, and threads, stencils, and templates for quilting.

Her work has been published through quilt books and magazines, and has been featured on *The Quilt Show*. Edyta's true passion and quilter's spirit shine through her classes, workshops, and presentations. She enjoys gardening and small-town living in Michigan, with her husband, Michael; three children; and loyal dog, Max. She connects with quilters everywhere through inspiring stories about the quilts she makes—and now those stories are quilting legends in the pages of *Reasons for Quilts*.

## Meet Judith Stern Friedman

Judy Friedman is a freelance writer and hobby quilter, who feels fortunate to be working at what she loves. Her entreé into the quilting industry began in the early 1990s, when she approached *American Patchwork and Quilting (APQ)* magazine (a *Better Homes & Gardens* publication) to write about 1930s kit quilts. The 200-word story evolved into a calling of writing profiles for dozens of visionary and inspiring quilt artists, fabric designers, and instructors—and Edyta Sitar shines among them.

When the two worked together on Edyta's profile for the April 2011 *APQ* issue, they discovered in each other compatible gentle spirits, who were somehow destined to deliver *Reasons for Quilts*.

Judy is a regular contributor to twice-annual issues of *Quilt Sampler* magazine, and has written for more than a dozen special interest books and magazines, primarily in crafts, decorating, and holiday celebrations. She also has written words behind countless successful promotional campaigns. Judy shares her expertise through writing workshops and university-level teaching.

When not at the computer keyboard, she spends time with her husband, Howard, and two daughters. She is a personal trainer and fitness instructor, and lives for restorative walks in the woods with the family's black lab, Kashi.

### Other books by Edyta Sitar:
- *Hop To It!* (Landauer, 2009), winner of the "2009 Midwest Book Award" in Crafts, Hobbies, and How-To by the Midwest Independent Publishers Association (MIPA); and winner of a silver award for "2009 Book of the Year" in Crafts and Hobbies by ForeWord Reviews
- *Friendship Triangles* (Landauer, 2009)
- *Friendship Strips and Scraps* (Landauer, 2010)

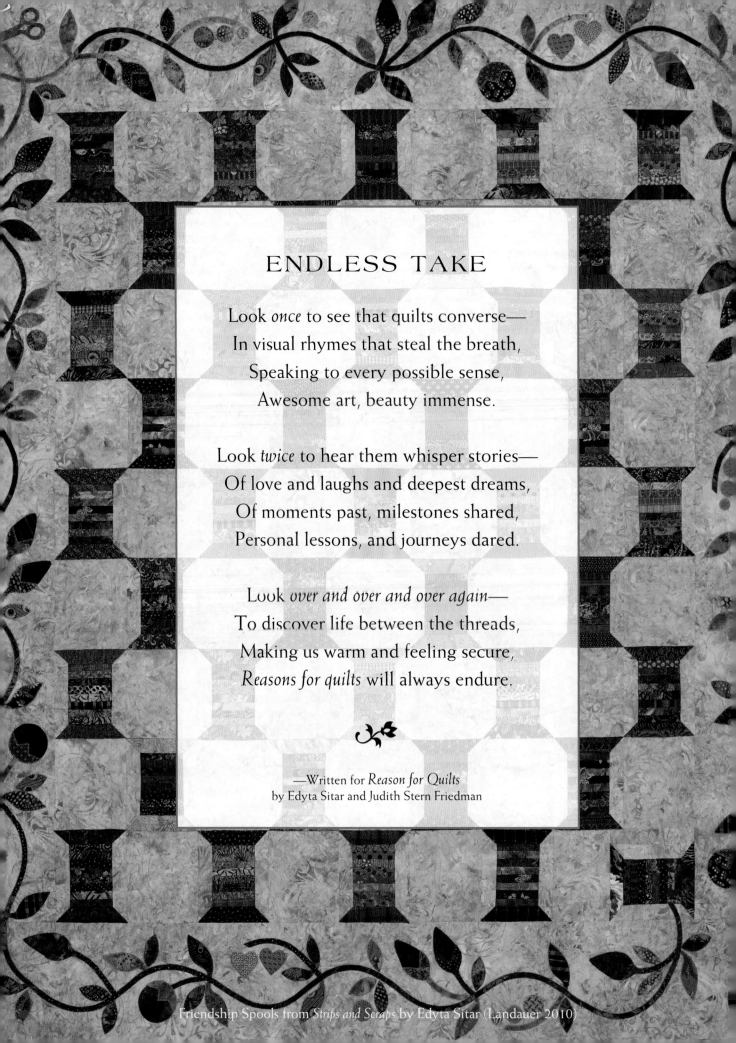

# ENDLESS TAKE

Look *once* to see that quilts converse—
In visual rhymes that steal the breath,
Speaking to every possible sense,
Awesome art, beauty immense.

Look *twice* to hear them whisper stories—
Of love and laughs and deepest dreams,
Of moments past, milestones shared,
Personal lessons, and journeys dared.

Look *over and over and over again*—
To discover life between the threads,
Making us warm and feeling secure,
*Reasons for quilts* will always endure.

—Written for *Reason for Quilts*
by Edyta Sitar and Judith Stern Friedman